East Bay Trails

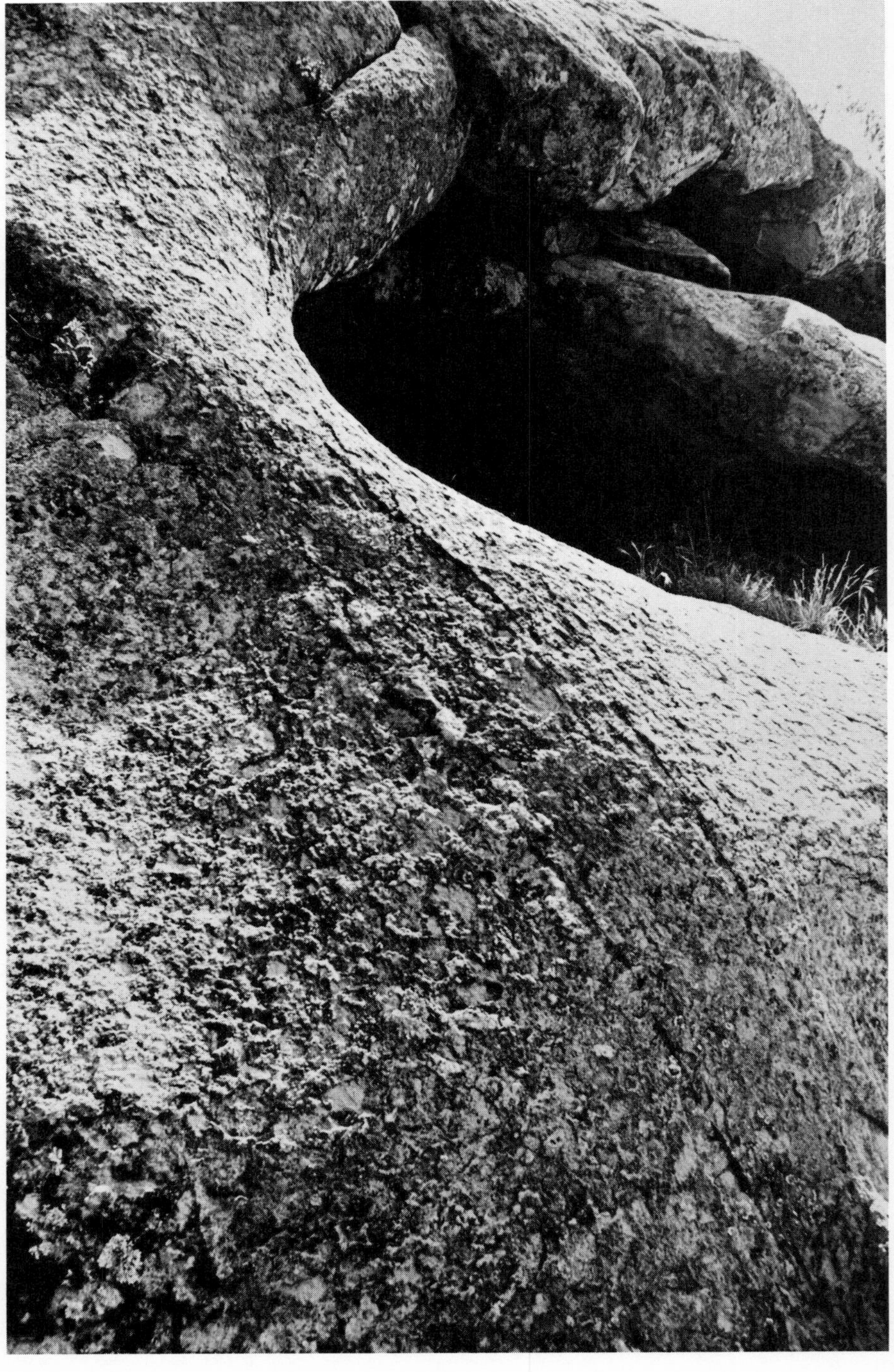

East Bay Trails

BOB NEWEY

a guide for hikers, runners, bicyclists & equestrians

Fourth Edition

fp

Footloose Press

Hayward

Break in storm, west from Mt. Diablo

First Edition, 1974
Second Edition, 1975
Third Edition, 1976

Published by Footloose Press
P.O. Box 3353
Hayward, CA 94540

Library of Congress Catalog Card: 80-69075
ISBN: 0-9605186-0-6

All maps, photographs and design by Bob Newey

Cover photo: Garin Regional Park Frontpiece: Sandstone, Las Trampas Back Cover: Donner Creek

Contents

Preface

Although this book is primarily intended to provide a convenient source of information, my hope is that it will do much more than that. I would like it to begin to turn people on to the richness of our big East Bay back yard, and to stimulate them to get out there and discover it for themselves. And perhaps in absorbing the intricate natural realities and the unique and subtle character of these places, they will become aware that this land is worth a great deal to us, a worth far beyond the measure of mere dollars. And they may also become aware that much of this land is being rapidly and needlessly destroyed to fill the pockets of a few individuals, that this destruction is directly related to many of our society's current problems—energy, pollution, urban decay, economic imbalance, etc.—and that we may stop this destruction only by becoming personally involved.

Outlying areas are being built up mostly because the land is relatively cheap. If all costs are considered, however, it is no bargain. Sprawl increases dependence on automobiles and lengthens commutes, wasting large amounts of energy and polluting the air. It destroys watersheds, increases run-off and silts up streams and reservoirs, wipes out wildlife habitat, and places a great burden on taxpayers, who often must pay for the duplication of services such as schools, police and fire protection, and utilities, which are already established in existing cities. For years, people, money and business have been deserting the older cities, leaving behind crumbling buildings, violent crime and alienated, strung-out people.

Of course we need more housing, but destruction of our hills is not the only way to get it. We can house the region's share of population growth by in-filling vacant land within cities, by rehabilitating old buildings, and by rebuilding some areas at higher density. It won't have to mean high rises and overcrowding, either. Some of the nicest neighborhoods of Oakland or Berkeley are densely populated and are desirable places to live. And building within existing cities will help reduce automobile dependence, energy needs and pollution.

Most of the local government officials who make the land-use decisions are heavily influenced by big contributions from developers and many are developers themselves. We should not be surprised that they frequently make decisions contrary to the best interests of the people.

There is a ray of hope in sight, though admittedly a dim one. The National Park Service recently completed a study to determine the feasibility of federal protection of the East Bay Ridgelands, an area which includes Alameda, Contra Costa and eastern Santa Clara counties. The study writers had expected it to recommend a greenline approach, one in which the federal government might make limited purchases of key parcels, but most of the land would remain in private hands with development controlled by a planning body representing all levels of government and interest groups. After months of delay, the study finally appeared with very weak recommendations, suggestive of some back-stage string pulling. The study will now be considered by Congress, and if they decide to put some weight behind the greenline concept, some of our hills may survive. But it won't happen without lots of popular support.

Personally, I don't really have much inclination to be an activist, but this land means too much to me to sit by and watch it being destroyed without expressing my disapproval. I may not make much difference but at least I'll feel better about myself. And if you have any of these same feelings for this land, whatever you can do to help—writing letters, attending hearings, donations, etc.—will be much appreciated, will put us a little closer to saving the land, and will make you feel good.

Since the first writing of this book in 1973-74, much has changed in the region and in my awareness of it. There have been many new trails and parks created, I've made a few new discoveries in old ones, and I've gained a much better understanding of the problems involved in the creation and management of parks and trails. A large portion of the book has been re-written to reflect these changes and bring it up-to-date.

Many people have helped with this revision, individuals and public employees, and I would like to thank them all. I would especially like to thank Bob Doyle, Harry Reeves, Bob Nuzum, Bob Cook, Ed Earl and Bob Pond, who provided lots of information, and Jana Olsen, who, in her several years as EBRPD Trails Coordinator got the regional trails system rolling, and who gave me loads of help with this book. And, most of all, I want to thank my family, without whose support this book could never have happened.

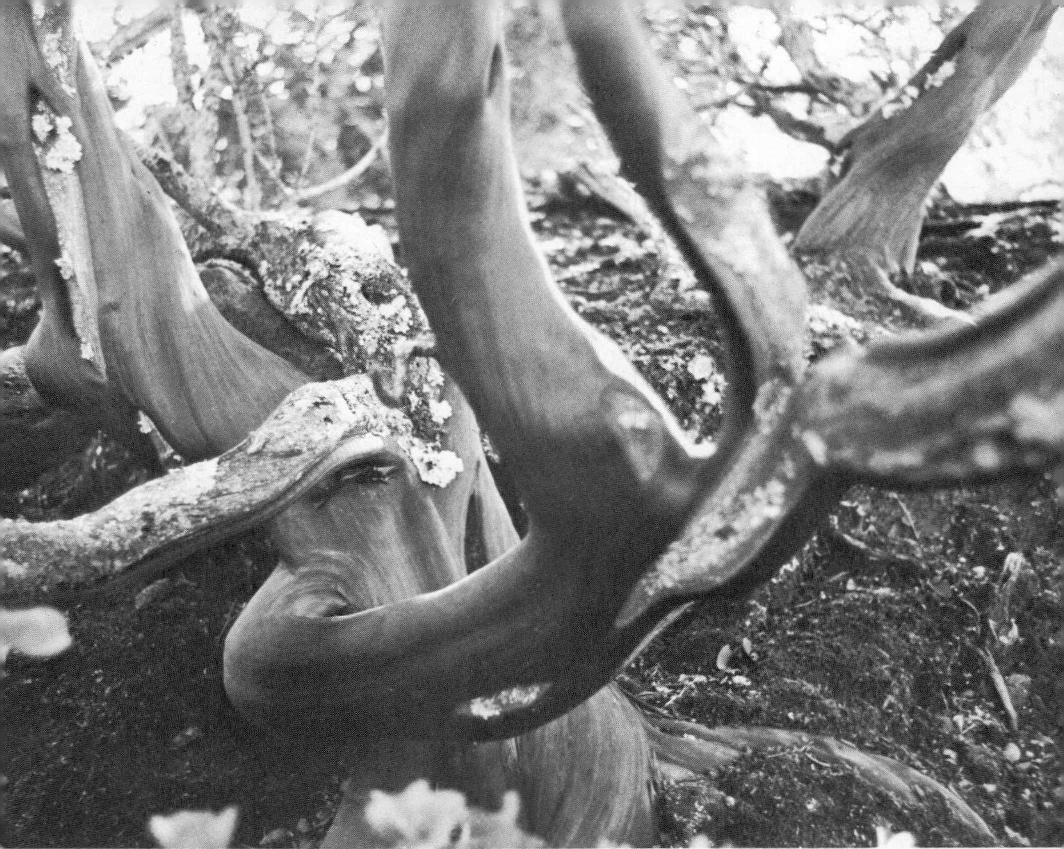

Organizations for open space, parks and trails in the East Bay:

Preserve Area Ridgelands Committee
4050 Poplar Avenue
Concord, CA 94521

Sierra Club, San Francisco Bay Chapter
6014 College Avenue
Oakland, CA 94618

Citizens for Urban Wilderness
4325 Mountain View Avenue
Oakland, CA 94605

People for Open Space
46 Kearny St.
San Francisco, CA 94108

Save Mount Diablo
P.O. Box 25
Concord, CA 94522

Save San Francisco Bay Assoc.
P.O. Box 925
Berkeley, CA 94701

East Bay Area Trails Council
11500 Skyline Blvd.
Oakland, CA 94619

Ohlone Audubon Society
22608 Linden Street
Hayward, CA 94541

See the random order of living earth,
hear its quiet,
smell its richness,
feel its realness,
open your heart to love.

Let it wash away the worries of the city,
your tensions and discomforts,
as you walk through woods and fields.

I. The Land

Introduction

If you like walking in the country and you are a Bay Area resident or visitor, and you are unfamiliar with the quiet places of the East Bay, then this book was written for you. Included here is a brief introduction to the natural and human history of the area, its rocks, climate, plants, animals, and people, and then a guide to trails of all kinds, trails for a casual stroll or for a strenuous hike, trails for running, trails for riding a horse or a bicycle.

1.7 million people live in the East Bay, an area about 40 miles square. For an urban area, it has an unusually large amount of land preserved semi-wild in parks. There are many places more spectacular, more scenic, or more remote than the East Bay hills, but none that I would admit to be more beautiful in their natural state. Beauty is where you look for it, and to say that one natural environment is better than another is like saying one race of men is better than another. Besides, the more spectacular places require a lot of traveling from the East Bay, but all of these trails are within an hour's drive, and there is surely at least one within a few minutes. You can go for a morning walk and be home for lunch, or go out in the evening and be home by dark.

The proximity of the trails to big cities has a special significance in these days of energy shortage. More and more people are looking for recreation that doesn't require much gas, and undoubtedly these trails will receive much more use in coming years. I occasionally find myself wondering if it is wise to encourage more people out onto the trails because the hills will surely become more crowded, footworn and littered. But I conclude that only by encouraging everyone to become familiar with the natural world will they care enough about their environment, both wild and urban, to save it from destruction. Our society must make some very basic changes to survive the future, and the changes must take place in the minds and hearts of each one of us. We must aim for life, not death, cooperation, not competition, conservation, not exploitation, love, not paranoia. Where can we better absorb these attitudes than from the rocks, the trees and birds, than by getting away from the constant hustle of city life and relaxing our minds, even if only for a few hours. It will take more than a walk in the woods to change the world, but we must start somewhere.

Most of the trails described here are in the East Bay Regional Park District (EBRPD) system, which covers most of the two counties. These parks range from highly developed parks with all kinds of recreational facilities to near wilderness. The East Bay Municipal Utility District

Vallejo
Benecia
Carquinez Straits
SAN PABLO BAY
Martinez Shoreline
80
680
4
Martinez
Point Pinole
Pinole
Pinole Cr
San Pablo Cr
Kennedy Grove
EBMUD Watershed
Wildcat Cr
Wildcat Canyon
Richmond
San Pablo Res.
Briones Res.
Briones
17
101
Geo. Miller
El Cerrito
Pt. Isabel
Tilden
24
Skyline
Lafayette Res.
Trail
U. C.
Berkeley
Sibley
Lafayette-Moraga
Trail
Huckleberry
24
Lake Temescal
13
Joaquin Miller
Redwood
80
Lake Merritt
OAKLAND
580
Upper San Leandro Res.
EBMUD
17
SAN FRANCISCO
Alameda
Crown Beach
San Leandro Bay
Anthony Chabot
Lake Chabot
San Leandro Cr
San Leandro
Castro Valley
SAN
San Leandro Marina
San Lorenzo Cr
FRANCISCO
280
Hayward Shoreline
BAY
92
San Mateo
Coyote H
101
84

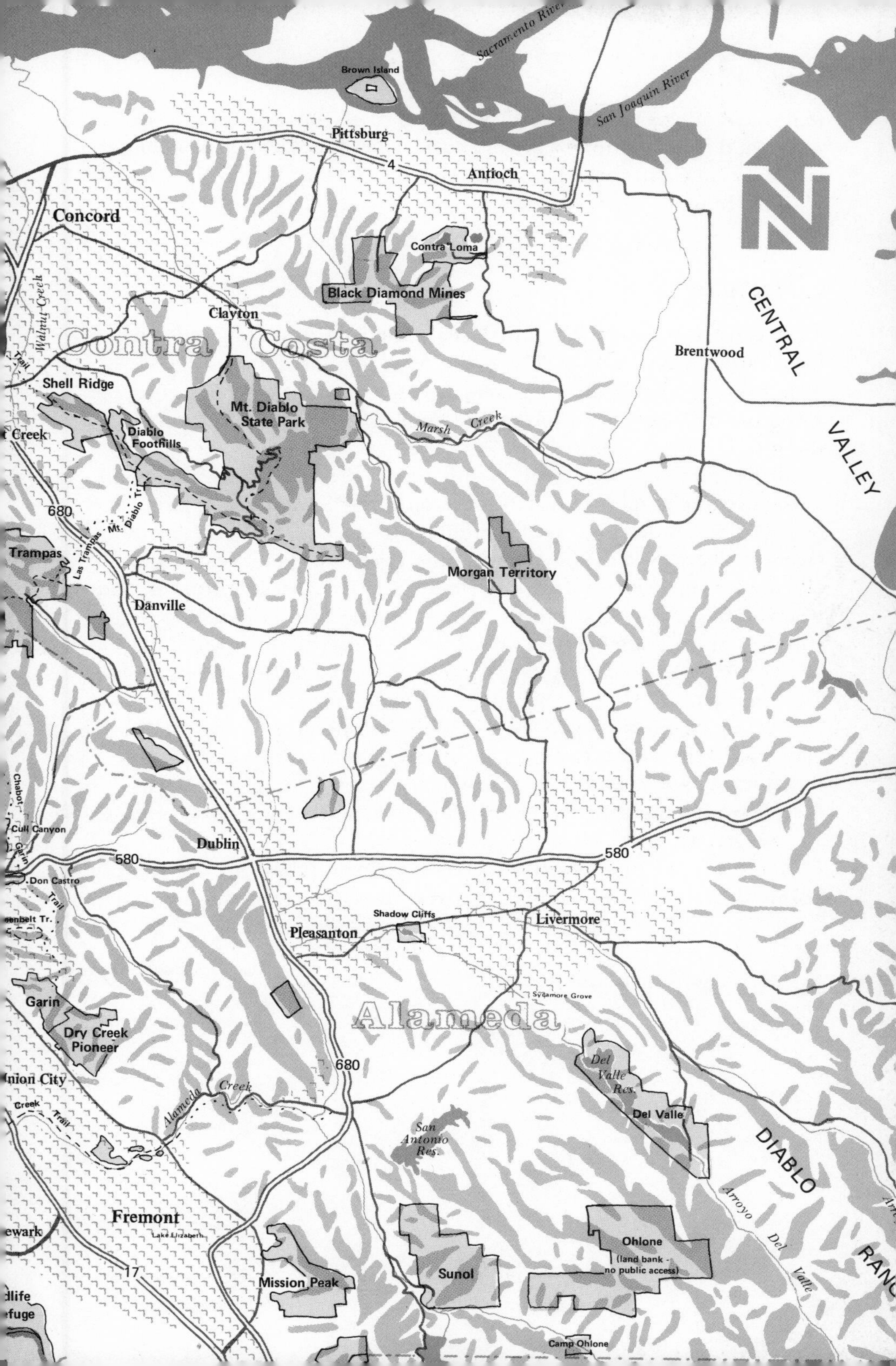

Sacramento River
Brown Island
San Joaquin River
Pittsburg
4
Antioch
Concord
Contra Loma
Black Diamond Mines
Walnut Creek
Clayton
Contra Costa
CENTRAL
VALLEY
Brentwood
Trail
Shell Ridge
Mt. Diablo State Park
Marsh Creek
Creek
Diablo Foothills
680
Las Trampas - Mt. Diablo Trail
Trampas
Morgan Territory
Danville
Chabot
Cull Canyon
Garin
Dublin
580
580
Don Castro
Trail
Greenbelt Tr.
Shadow Cliffs
Pleasanton
Livermore
Sycamore Grove
Alameda
Garin
Dry Creek Pioneer
680
Union City
Alameda Creek
Creek Trail
Del Valle Res.
Del Valle
San Antonio Res.
DIABLO
RANGE
Arroyo Del Valle
Fremont
Lake Elizabeth
Newark
17
Ohlone
(land bank - no public access)
Mission Peak
Sunol
Wildlife Refuge
Camp Ohlone

(EBMUD) allows public use of two of its reservoirs and trails in its watershed lands. Other public open space lands covered here include city parks, a California State Park, University lands, and a National Wildlife Refuge.

Climate

Because it is near the Pacific Ocean, the East Bay shows a lot of local variation in weather. There is often a dramatic change (20 or 30 degrees) over a few miles. The reason is the exposure to ocean breezes along the bay shore, and the shelter from them that the hills provide to the interior.

In the summer, fog usually builds up off the coast, blowing inland in the evening and burning off in the morning. Sometimes it never gets beyond the Golden Gate and sometimes it reaches to Mt. Diablo. Often it clears over the bay, leaving the Berkeley Hills wreathed in clouds. It is not exactly fog; low clouds is a better description. In and near the fog it is cool, damp and breezy, while further inland it is hot and dry. Since it almost never rains in the summer, the grassy hills become dry and golden brown. Most of the streams dry up and fires are common.

In the fall, the ocean fog subsides and temperatures near the bay may rise to the 100's. Later on, cool clear days are broken by occasional haze, clouds and rain. A few of the trees turn color and drop their leaves (some oaks, sycamore, buckeye, and poison oak), but most are evergreens.

In the winter, the rain storms start in earnest. These are cyclonic storms–like a hurricane but much less violent. Thunder and lightning

A rare sight– snow in Tilden

are rare, and snow almost never falls except in the highest hills. The rain storms may line up one after another for weeks. In between storms it is often very clear, temperatures varying from comfortable to freezing. Low, cold, dense tule fogs may spread from the Central Valley to cover the eastern valleys of the area. East of the Berkeley Hills, it often freezes at night, but it seldom freezes near the bay. The hills become green with fresh grass and the creeks become muddy torrents. Springtime seems to come in mid-winter as the fields and orchards become covered with yellow mustards.

In the spring come warmer temperatures, fewer storms and many beautifully clear days. Spring wildflowers cover the hills with color. This is the best time of the year for walking these trails, though all seasons are good. Late in the spring, the ocean fog makes its appearance again, ushering in the summer.

Rocks

The East Bay lies on one of the geologically most active parts of the earth's surface, where two huge pieces of the earth's crust are grinding against each other. The Pacific plate, which underlies most of the

Pacific Ocean, is moving northwest from its source in the East Pacific rise, and being carried down into the earth's mantle along the deep sea trenches which line the coast of Asia from the Aleutians to New Zealand. On the California coast it slides against the North American plate along the San Andreas fault system. This system includes not only the long San Andreas Fault itself, but also other major faults which take up much of the movement. Two of these in the East Bay are the Hayward Fault along the west base of the Berkeley Hills and the Calaveras Fault through Sunol and San Ramon Valleys. Both are active and continue to cause earthquakes.

Let's imagine going back a hundred million years or so, when dinosaurs were running about. The movement of the Pacific plate was at that time toward the coast and bending down into the earth along a trench, the site of the present East Bay. To the east, lightweight molten rock floated from the descending crust up into the depths of a low folded mountain range, solidifying to form the granite core of the Sierra Nevada. Sediments washed from the mountains and lava from submerged volcanoes piled into the trench. These rocks were crumpled between the crustal plates, became metamorphic, and about 75 million years ago (late Jurassic) were uplifted here and there as the beginnings of the coast ranges. Today these are the oldest rocks of the East Bay, the Franciscan formation. They are colorful rocks, red, brown, gray and green; chert, sandstone and serpentine. Later trench sediments became shales and sandstones with fossil shells.

Far to the west, two oceanic crustal plates were spreading apart, and molten rock from below was welling up between them and solidifying to form a mid-ocean ridge. This ridge was moving toward the coast and about 30 million years ago ploughed into the trench and stuck there. With the descending crust no longer dragging it down, the trench floated up and raised hills out of the water, which retreated to approximate the present coast about 12 million years ago (end of Miocene). After the ridge hit the trench, the ocean floor began moving northwest (as it still does), forming the San Andreas fault system at its contact with the continental plate. The Santa Cruz Mountains and Point Reyes were then located near the present Mexican border, and have since slid along the coast to their present locations as part of the Pacific plate. The hills were worn down to plains, except for a long range where the bay is now. Sediments from these hills washed onto the plains east of them, sometimes burying the lush tropical forest and making coal. These rocks are mostly shales, sandstones and conglomerates. Some of the layers (the Orinda formation) contain fossils of large mammals such

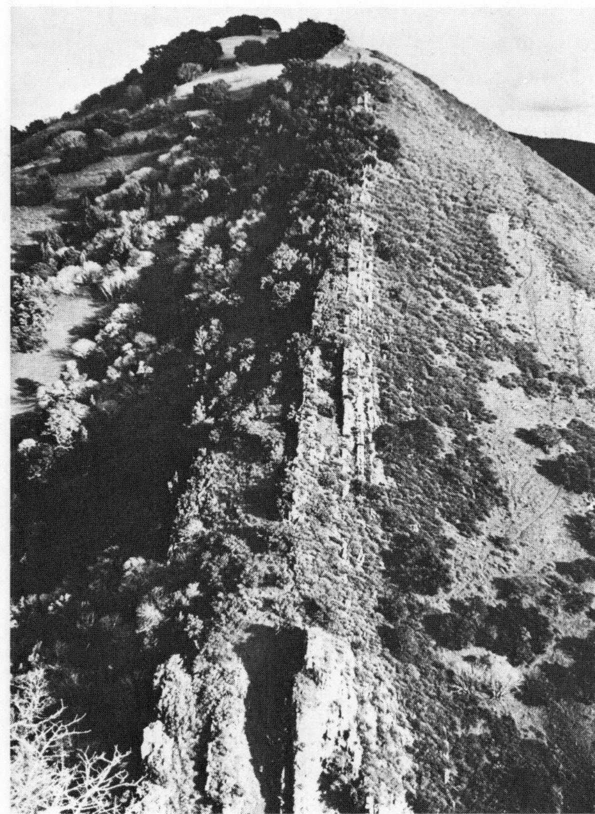

Vertical sandstone beds, South Gate, Mt. Diablo

as mastodons and camels. Volcanoes poured out lava where the Berkeley Hills now stand (Grizzly Peak, Round Top), and showered ash on the region.

About 5 million years ago, the region was strongly folded, faulted and uplifted, producing mountains roughly where they are today. These were worn down to low hills, and the combined Sacramento and San Joaquin Rivers cut a canyon through them, forming Carquinez Straits and the Golden Gate. Another period of faulting and uplift took place about a million years ago. The melting of the Ice Age glaciers caused the sea level to rise and flood a long valley, producing the bay.

Though this brings us back to the present, the movements of the earth are by no means finished. These processes are slowly going on right now, and will probably still be going on long after man has disappeared from the earth.

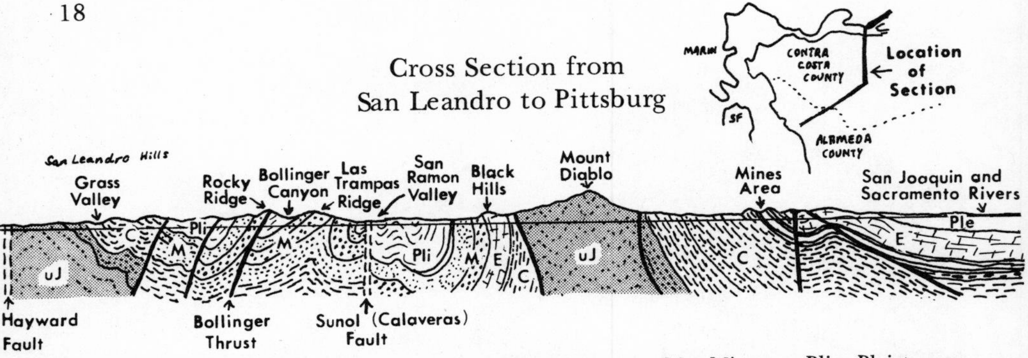

uJ = upper Jurassic (Franciscan), C = Cretaceous, E = Eocene, M = Miocene, Pli = Pleistocene

The cross section above shows some representative subsurface formations. Bay mud rests on Franciscan bedrock on the bay plain (not shown), Franciscan rock low on the west slope of the Berkeley Hills gives way to complexly folded and faulted younger shale and sandstone, pierced by a core of Franciscan rock forming Mt. Diablo (and the Mt. Hamilton Range to the south), and beds of younger rocks dip under the recent sediments of the Central Valley.

Plants

Certain plants (and animals) seem to like each other's company and are often found growing together as a community, while a short distance away, another set of quite different plants may be found together, another community. These communities form a living mosaic whose pattern is determined by local climatic variations due to wind, coastal fog, rainshadow caused by hills, moisture collecting in canyon bottoms, and shady north or sunny south facing slopes. Other determinants are the fertility of the soil, frequent fires, and the works of man—lumbering, farming, livestock raising and city building.

On the tidelands of the bay it is too salty for most land plants, so a few grasses (cordgrass) and succulents (pickleweed) which have adapted to salty conditions grow above the mud flats, forming the *salt marsh* community.

Not salt, but the low oxygen content of stagnant freshwater wet areas allows tall rushes and cattails to grow—the *freshwater marsh.*

On shady northern hillsides grows *broadleaf evergreen forest.* The predominant tree, and one of the most common in the area, is the California bay (or laurel). It gives a spicy fragrance to the woods. Break one of its narrow shiny green leaves; its smell is unmistakeable. The tree is tall and rounded with a heavy trunk, though it may be only a big

Poison oak

shrub on exposed ridges. Other plants of this community include madrone, with its thin red peeling bark and smooth tan skin underneath, coast live oak (see oak woodland, below), and poison oak. The latter is a beautiful shrub or vine, but one to avoid at all costs if you are allergic to it (most people are). Its oval leaves are dark green and shiny, in groups of three. In summer and fall they turn brilliant red. It is very common, and is found throughout the East Bay. Its effects are like those of poison ivy—a miserable itching, stinging rash appearing several days after contact. Avoid getting it by avoiding the plant, by bathing as soon as you get home (some recommend strong soap like Fels-Naptha), and by washing your clothes before wearing them again.

In limited areas along the tops of the Berkeley Hills and around the EBMUD reservoirs, there is *closed cone pine forest,* with Monterey pine. These trees have been planted, though they are natives to nearby regions. It has needles in bunches of three, in dark clusters on widely spaced branches, with a rounded crown when mature.

In the southern Berkeley Hills there is *redwood forest.* The coast redwood is a beautiful tree, familiar to most Californians. Its needles are about ½″ long, dark green and flat. The bark is reddish and fibrous. It has tiny cones. Old redwoods grow to be gigantic trees, but none in the East Bay are much more than 100 years old since they were all cut for lumber in the early days. Even so, many have trunks 3 ft. in diameter. Beneath the trees, sword fern is plentiful.

Also common in the Berkeley Hills is *eucalyptus forest.* These trees are not native, but were brought from Australia around 1910 and planted for lumber. The wood turned out to be not much good for anything. The trees have narrow dull green leaves, thick shaggy peeling trunks, and small conical seed pods with a spicy fragrance. A freak cold spell in December 1972 killed much of the hilltop forests. Afraid that the dry leaves would feed fires, endangering homes in the hills, large areas of forest were cleared, leaving ugly barren hillsides, some of which have already sprouted small groves of these fast growing trees. The EBRPD plans to eventually clear most of the eucalyptus from the parks and replant with native trees.

On hillsides within reach of the ocean fog, there grows *coastal scrub,* characterized by the common shrub, coyote bush. It grows head high and has small (½″), round, dull green leaves, and in the fall it becomes covered with small white bits of fluff. It is accompanied by bush monkey flower, shrubby lupine, poison oak, poison hemlock, and vine thickets of blackberry and thimbleberry.

A closely related community, *sage scrub,* is found on the dry interior hills (Black Diamond Mines, Sunol), with California sagebrush, black sage, yerba santa and bush monkey flower.

On dry, rocky ridges further inland, or higher than coastal scrub, grows *chaparral.* The characteristic plant is a shrub, chamise. It has shaggy reddish branches encrusted with pale green lichens, and small (¼″) dark green needles. From a distance it is very dark, hence the naming of the Black Hills south of Mt. Diablo. In May, it is covered with tiny white flowers which turn brown in the summer. Other chaparral plants include mountain mahogany, toyon, hollyleaf cherry, coffeeberry, scrub oak, and many species of ceanothus and manzanita. These plants have small leathery moisture conserving leaves and long roots reaching into cracks in the rock, characteristics which well adapt them to the dry summers.

Much of the East Bay hills are covered with *oak woodland.* The coast live oak is the most common tree of the East Bay and it dominates the oak woodland toward the bay. It has a thick rough trunk with wide spreading crooked limbs. Its leaves are dark shiny green spoons with tiny points around the edge. They stay green and on the tree year round. Two similar oaks are common toward the valley, the interior live oak and the canyon live oak. Deciduous oaks are more prevalent on the interior hills. They include the black oak with pointed lobed leaves, the valley oak with rounded lobed leaves, and the blue oak with slightly lobed leaves. The California buckeye is found in oak woodland as well as other communities. It is a small rounded tree with a grayish trunk. In June, it is covered with plumes of white flowers. The fruit is like a chestnut, a 2″ round, shiny brown nut within a husk.

On Mt. Diablo and south of Livermore there is *foothill pine* woodland, with digger pine, a wispy tree with a forked trunk, a rounded crown and long grayish green needles. It grows with chaparral and oaks. North of Mt. Diablo, it is replaced by the Coulter pine, a scrawny tree with dark green needles, a brown trunk and heavy clawed cones.

Large areas of the interior hills are grassland. Originally these plants were mostly perennials—bunch grasses. These grasses don't recover easily from grazing, and taste better to cows than annuals like foxtail and wild oats, many of which have been introduced from Europe, and as a result, the latter have largely replaced the native bunch grasses. Thistles are common in grassland, and many kinds of wildflowers bloom in the spring, including California poppy, Mariposa lily, lupine, monkey flower, and buttercup. Mustards bloom in the winter, and tarweed blooms late in the summer.

Along streams throughout the region grows *riparian woodland.* A tree characteristic of this community is the western sycamore, a big awkward tree with a mottled cream colored trunk and big star shaped leaves. Willows, alders and other moisture loving plants often crowd the banks.

Animals

When the first white men settled in the East Bay, grizzly bears and wolves were common, as well as large herds of elk and antelope. Though these animals have long been gone and others nearly eliminated by the press of civilization, the area still supports lots of wild animals, far too many to list here. I'll just mention a few of the more obvious ones.

Of the countless insects, perhaps the most startling to meet is the tarantula, found on Mt. Diablo and similar areas. Its sting can be very painful but not really dangerous. Mosquitos and flies are seldom a problem.

Small rattlesnakes are sometimes encountered. They may be confused with gopher snakes or king snakes which are more common. Garter snakes, salamanders and newts, and frogs are plentiful in wet areas.

Of the many birds in the area, the Steller's jay is the one most likely to be seen and heard in the woods. It has a loud raucous call, and little fear of humans. It is a robin-sized bird, shiny blue, with a crest. In brush, the scrub jay is more common. Plump little California quail will often be heard rustling about in the brush or may be seen running across the trail. It is gray and brown striped with a plume atop its head. In any of the hills, especially the drier ones you will see turkey vultures.

Turkey vulture

Mule deer

These large black scavengers float in endless circles, rarely moving their wings. They are all black and gray except for their naked red head. Another large soaring bird you may see is the red tailed hawk. It is brown with a fanned reddish tail. A few other common birds are the mourning dove, red shafted flicker, robin, red-winged blackbird, black headed grosbeak, Bullock's oriole, Oregon junco, house finch, towhees, chicadees, goldfinches, titmice, and bushtits. On the bay shores, egrets, sandpipers, gulls and terns may be seen, and in the fall, ducks, coots, and Canada geese stop by.

The loud shrill chirp of the California ground squirrel is commonly heard on grassy hillsides. He may be seen standing erect like a prairie dog at the entrance to his burrow. He is mottled brownish-gray, about 10″ tall, with an un-bushy tail. Ground squirrels are a pest to ranchers, who trap or poison them. Mule (black-tailed) deer are commonly seen, if you go quietly. They easily frighten and go crashing through the brush in graceful leaps. They are beautiful animals, about 3′ tall at the shoulder, with a black tail on a white rump and long "mule" ears. Usually they are seen singly or in small groups, but one Christmas Eve, just at sunset, I came across a herd of more than 100 of them grazing on Rocky Ridge. Mountain lions occasionally wander through the area, but they are rare. Wildacts live in wooded ravines, but they are very shy, and gray foxes and coyotes inhabit the brushy hills, but it is extremely unlikely that you will encounter any of these predators while hiking, since they are most active at night, and the years of being hunted by men have made them very cautious. Other mammals include rabbits, rats, mice, gophers, moles, shrews, skunks, badgers, weasels, raccoons, ringtails, opposums, and bats.

People

Before the arrival of Europeans to the East Bay, the Ohlone (or Costanoan) Indians lived here peacefully, in harmony with their environment. Early observers characterized these Indians as culturally and intellectually the most primitive of America, a judgment which showed great misunderstanding of a very different way of life adapted to a very different natural environment than that from which they had come. Food was relatively plentiful here, but very seasonal, best suited to a nomadic lifestyle of hard work during several short harvest seasons and not much to do the rest of the time. Thus they were seen to be lazy and primitive, and also timid because they knew little of greed and violence, so familiar to the Europeans.

They ate shellfish from the bay, deer and small game, and acorn meal ground in stone mortars. They went naked most of the time, and in cold weather wore skins or covered themselves with mud to keep warm. The men made a ritual of sitting in sweat houses (steam baths) followed by a cold swim to purify their bodies. They usually lived out their lives without traveling far from home. Around the shores of the Bay they built shell mounds—piles of discarded shells, pottery and tools, as well as the graves of their dead.

When the Spanish missionaries came beginning with the Portola expedition exploring the area in 1769 and the De Anza expedition with the first settlers in 1776, the Indians were forced into slavery and a strange new religion. In the East Bay, Mission San Jose de Guadalupe was founded in 1797 in what is now part of Fremont. Though it became one of the most prosperous of the missions, for the Indians there as everywhere in California, it was a disaster. Their spirits broken by oppression, most of them died of common European diseases to which they had no immunity.

In 1821, Mexico won its independence and took control of California. They didn't like the autonomy that the missions enjoyed, and in 1833 returned the mission lands to the state, freeing the Indians to live in poverty as servants or ranchhands, or, if they chose to return to their wild ways, to be hunted and killed as outlaws.

The Spanish rewarded members of the early expeditions with huge land grants. One of the first was made to Luis Maria Peralta in 1820. It encompassed all of the bay plain from Albany to San Leandro and was later divided between his four sons, Ygnacio, Antonio, Vicente and Jose Domingo.

The first English speaking settler of the East Bay was Robert Livermore who jumped ship from the British Navy in 1822 and obtained the Rancho Las Positas in the Livermore Valley.

The first American here was an enigmatic character named John Marsh. He was a moody, temperamental man who was disliked by most but was a friend of the Indians. He came to California in 1836, and posing as a doctor, was able to buy a large rancho northeast of Mt. Diablo. He became prosperous and along with his friend in Sacramento, John Sutter, he wrote and encouraged many of his eastern acquaintances to migrate to California. His good fortune didn't last, however, and he was killed by squatters on his ranch in 1856. His stone house still stands on Marsh Creek Road.

During the Mexican-American War, in 1846, Americans in California took control, declared a short-lived republic, then annexed to the United States. Soon Americans stampeded into the state for the gold rush and everything changed practically overnight. The exploding population of gold seekers overwhelmed the old ways of the ranchos. Like most landowners, the Peraltas soon had more squatters than they could handle, and lost or sold most of their land.

One of those squatters, Horace W. Carpentier, one night led a gang of men to Vicente Peralta's house and pressured him to lease him land which he laid out in city blocks. He secretly got Oakland incorporated in 1852, set himself up in control of the city's waterfront and much of the railroad and ferry boat transportation to and from it, and was fraudulantly elected mayor. His hold on the city lasted for years until the leader of a reform movement, Dr. Samuel Merritt, became the city's mayor.

In the early days, Oakland developed as a seaport and railroad terminal for the lumber cut from the redwood forest just over the hill. It soon became the economic center of the East Bay. Berkeley was built around the University of California which was established in 1867. Richmond was developed as a rival port to Oakland by a real estate promoter, Augustin S. Macdonald, who persuaded the Santa Fe Railroad to build a line to Richmond to compete with the Southern Pacific. Pittsburg was the center of the coal mining industry in the nearby hills. Around the turn of the century, steel mills were built there, beginning the heavy industrial development of the north Contra Costa shoreline. The rest of the area was mostly large ranches and small villages, raising cattle, wheat, and later fruits, nuts and wine grapes.

During World War II, many thousands of workers came to work in the shipyards in Oakland and Richmond and the region experienced another spurt of growth which has continued to the present day as the agricultural valleys have one by one become suburban cities with freeways, shopping centers and tract homes. At the same time, the older cities have become ghettos.

Today the East Bay is a mixture of people from many backgrounds. Large numbers of Mexican-Americans and other Latins live throughout the area, but especially East Oakland, Hayward and Union City. In San Leandro, Hayward and San Pablo there are many descendants of Portugese settlers who pioneered these areas. In Oakland there is a smaller version of San Francisco's chinatown, and chinese, filipinos and other orientals are very much a part of the region. Large areas of Oakland, Berkeley, Richmond and Pittsburg have predominantly black populations. And of course there is the white majority which tend more toward the suburbs. Because of the rapid growth of the East Bay in recent years, one characteristic shared by all ethnic groups is that more likely than not they haven't been here too long.

Hiking

Just walking can be a most enjoyable way to spend one's time. People do it for many reasons. Some charge up mountains in a display of endurance, trying to prove their strength. Others poke along studying every plant, observing every bird. Some hike to keep fit, some to enjoy the scenery, some to converse with companions, some to be alone. Whatever your motivation, you will find that your experiences will be more intense and meaningful if you really tune in to, and become a part of, your surroundings. Become aware of the whole picture at once, the land and plants and animals all fitting together, and how you fit in too. Do what you can to stay comfortable, but if you are not don't let it bring you down.

Now for a little more practical advice. It is a good idea to carry water on the longer hikes, as clean water is usually not available. Don't drink water from streams unless you know it is pure; many are contaminated by livestock. Be prepared for unexpected temperature changes. Watch out for poison oak (see p. 19). In many of the parks you will encounter herds of cows and sometimes bulls. They usually won't bother you, but it is a good idea to detour around them when possible. It isn't easy to get lost in this area, but it would be wise to carry a topographic map in the wilder areas. Hiking alone can be risky, especially for women. I do it myself now and then, and some of my most memorable experiences have been while solo hiking, but the possible consequences are worth considering. The East Bay is really a pretty gentle environment compared to most places—you don't have to worry much about extreme heat or cold, lightning or tornadoes, dangerous animals or restless natives. I really feel safer on these trails than on lots of city streets.

You may wish to combine hiking with camping and there are some nice places to camp in the area. Anthony Chabot Regional Park, Sunol Regional Wilderness, Del Valle Regional Park and Mt. Diablo State Park all have family camping areas and Sunol has campsites for backpackers.

When I was a kid in the fifties there were few parks, few hikers, and most ranchers were tolerant, so we just climbed fences and went where we wanted. But those days are gone, and trespassing is no longer appropriate. The EBRPD is now expanding its regional trail system and in many places must obtain right-of-way across private land, which is very difficult without the owner's cooperation. Climbing fences will only arouse their hostility and, in the long run, cut our choices of places to hike. Let's show respect for all of the land, private and public. Wherever you hike, please don't litter, stray from the trail, leave gates open, let dogs chase cattle or wildlife or be careless with fire.

A New Concept in Trails

Someday in the future, we may be able to get on a trail a short distance from home or transit and walk, ride or cycle to parks and cities anywhere in the East Bay. The Regional Park District has planned such a trail network and they have already put a great deal of effort into planning trails, preparing environmental impact reports, acquiring rights of way, and trail building. Several of these trails are now complete—the East Bay Skyline National Recreational Trail, the Alameda Creek Trail, the Lafayette-Moraga Trail, and portions of other regional trails.

These new trails represent a new concept in trails. Instead of being confined to park land, as most trails have been in the past, these regional trails will pass through both public and private lands and will connect the parks with each other and with population centers. Although routes are being selected that generally avoid development, in many places the trails will go through urban areas and will greatly facilitate non-motorized transportation to work, school or shopping as well as recreation.

These new trails will open a lot of new choices for recreation. With the proposed addition of backpacking camps at appropriate intervals, it will be possible to walk or ride for several days and cover long distances, to have a wilderness-type experience in an urban region.

In planning these trails, the park district has often encountered opposition from people living near the proposed route. They have expressed fears of many problems with trail users—vandalism, fire, etc.—but in a recent park district study of two existing trails through residential areas, the Lafayette-Moraga Trail and the Alameda Creek Trail, it was found that most people living adjacent to the trail liked having it there, and reported very few problems with trail users. Many of the feared problems are actually lessened by public use of an area because people are around to report or prevent destructive behavior.

One part of the system with high priority with the park district, and which is well on its way to completion, is a long trail which has been informally called the "Golden Loop." It will include part of the existing Skyline Trail, EBMUD Watershed trails and will connect the following parks: Tilden, Briones, Mt. Diablo, Las Trampas, Redwood and back to Tilden, a loop of 65 miles or so. There will also be a trail cutting across the loop from Briones through Lafayette and Moraga to Las Trampas, much of which is also already in place. Other trails currently being worked on will extend the Skyline Trail from Chabot to Garin parks and the Alameda Creek Trail through Niles Canyon to the town of Sunol. Many other trails are shown on the park district's master plan, as well as on the State Trail Plan which includes a proposed connection between Mt. Diablo and Henry Coe State Parks.

It takes a great deal of energy and work to make real trails out of lines on a map, and much of the credit for our success in expanding our trail system belongs to the efforts of trail user groups which have worked together as the East Bay Area Trails Council. A great deal of thanks is due both the citizens and the public employees who have made possible the trails we now have, and if we all give our support and encouragement, we should be able to fill in the gaps and take pride in a wonderful trail network.

Notes on Trail Descriptions

For each route described, I have given some figures at the beginning to give you an idea of the length and difficulty of the trail. First is the distance, which was measured on topographic maps, and though not exact, is accurate to a tenth of a mile or so. Second is the elevation gain, also obtained from topo maps, and it represents the sum of all the climbing, not just the difference between the highest and lowest points, rounded off to the nearest 100 feet. In previous editions I also included the duration of the hike, but decided that it didn't really mean much because walking speeds vary so, and it didn't relate to runners, bicyclists and equestrians.

In the descriptions, when I say "a trail branches left," I don't mean that you are to follow that trail, but that you should stay to the right. I have picked these routes to make interesting hikes, but also to cover most of the trails of the area. Don't hesitate to change them; your route will probably suit you better than mine. Driving directions are given with downtown Oakland as the starting point.

Key to Trail Maps

one mile

one kilometer

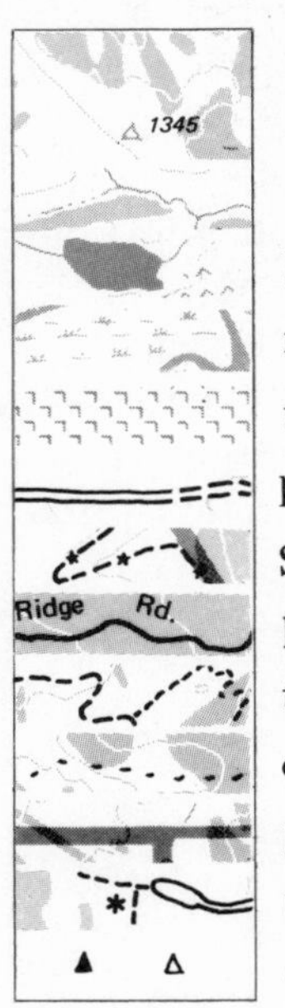

shaded relief with 200 ft. contours
peak, elevation in feet
stream; intermittent/year round
lake
marsh
urban development
public paved/dirt road
Skyline Trail
paved trail, no motor vehicles
trail: wide/narrow
cross country route
park/watershed boundary
trail access point
campground; family/group

II. The Trails

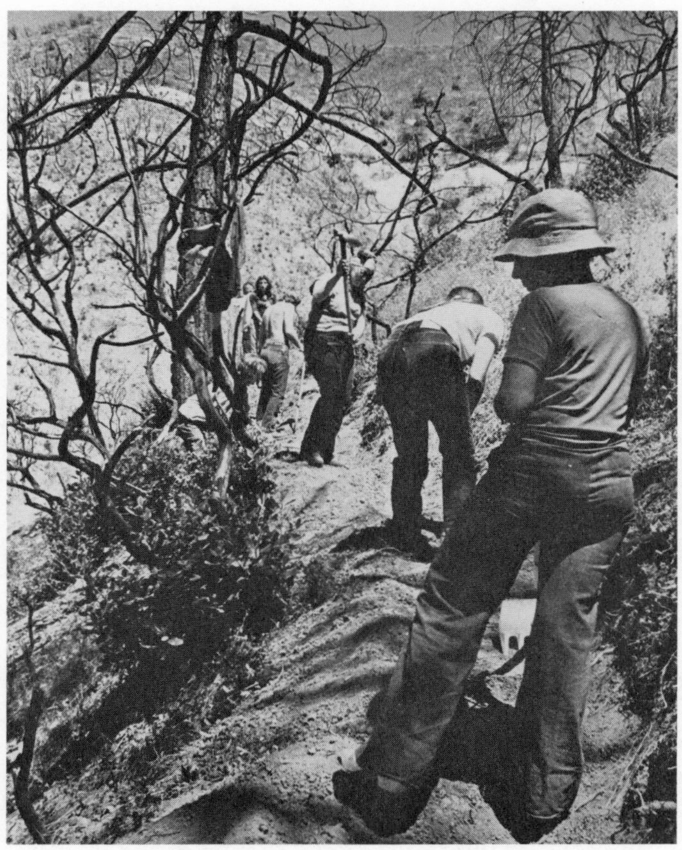

Volunteer trail builders, Back Canyon, Mt. Diablo

1. By the Bay

Martinez Shoreline

Martinez Shoreline

Shorebirds and marshes, little boats and big ships passing by on the river, green grass and playground, an old ferry and marina, the industrial side of the old town of Martinez—these are some of the sights and sounds of the recently opened (1979) Martinez Regional Shoreline.

The park includes about a mile and a half of mudflats and marshes along the Martinez shore of the Carquinez Straits. Enclosed by the park, but not part of it, is the Martinez Marina and fishing pier. Gravel paths and bridges make it easy to explore the marshes without getting wet feet.

To get there, take Freeway 24 to Walnut Creek, I-680 north, Highway 4 west to Martinez, Alhambra Ave. north through town, right on Escobar and left on Ferry St.

As a very worthwhile side trip, stop and look around John Muir's home, a national historic site that has been nicely restored. It is located on Alhambra Ave. at Highway 4.

Point Pinole

Point Pinole Regional Shoreline is a unique spot, one with lots of subtle charm. Stately eucalyptus forests surround golden meadows and end abruptly in crumbling cliffs and pebble beach washed by little bay waves. Green salt marsh oozing with unseen life is nourished by the rising and falling tides. Colors are often muted by fog drifting through the trees but there are always colorful smells of the sea, eucalyptus and fragrant weeds.

Before 1971, when the park first opened, the point was occupied by an explosives plant. The buildings have all been torn down, but many storage bunkers remain. The point is nearly flat, the highest hill being just over 100 feet. Inland, it is eucalyptus forest and grassland; along the shore are narrow beaches, seacliffs, salt marsh, and a new fishing pier opened in 1977, served by a shuttle service from the parking lot.

To get there, take I-80 north through Richmond to Hilltop Dr. Go left, then turn right on San Pablo Ave., left on Atlas Rd., then left on Giant Highway to the park entrance. AC Transit has special summer bus service weekends from the Richmond BART Station.

Around the Point

4.0 mi./100 ft. climb

This route leads around the shores of the point through eucalyptus, salt marsh, and along the beach. From the parking lot, follow the road along the tracks, over them on a bridge, and turn right at the first opportunity. Go across Pinole Meadow and through the forest, wind sighing in the leaves. When the bay comes into view, follow a path to the shore and then head toward the point between salt marsh and muddy beach, enjoying the tranquility of lapping waves and circling gulls (at high tide, take the dirt road around the south side of Whittell Marsh). Soon

West shore, near the point

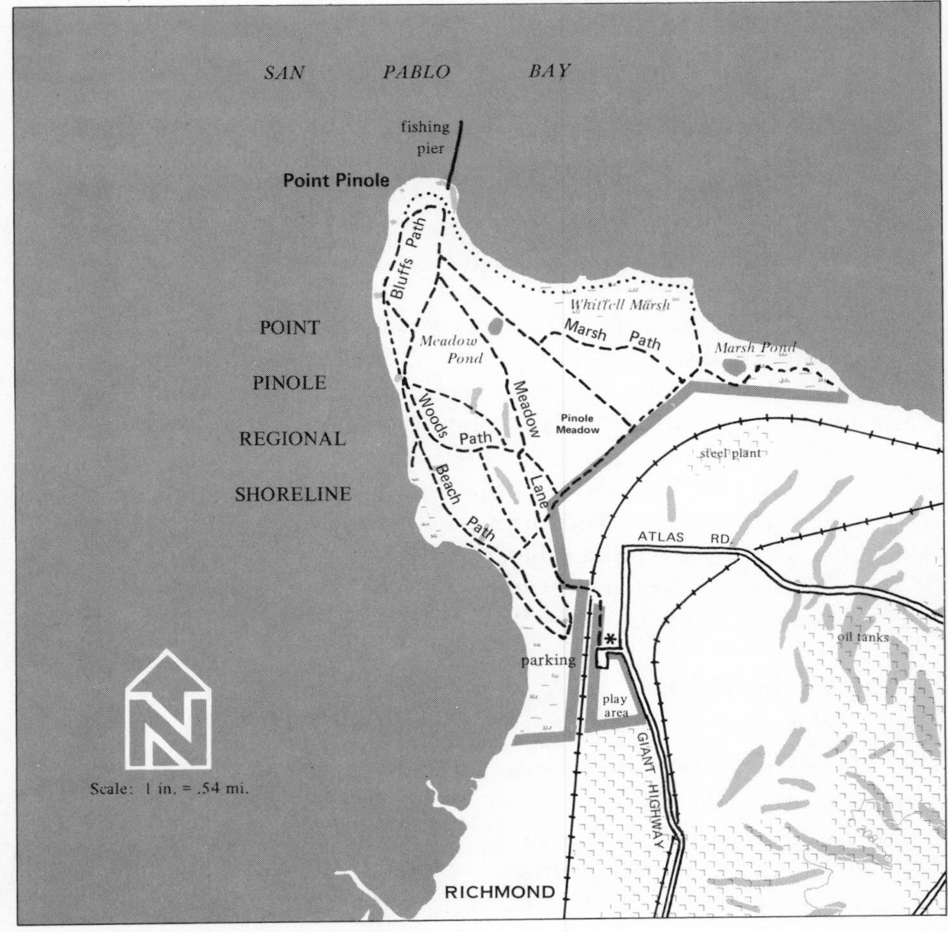

there is a sandy beach littered with broken shells, jellyfish and assorted debris. Pass the pier and round the tip of the point along the edge of a cliff. There is a wide panorama of the bay backed by Marin hills. Follow the shore above a rocky beach strewn with interesting junk, until it is interrupted by a small patch of salt marsh. Then go left on a footpath to a grassy hilltop overlooking Richmond. Cut across the fields to the bridge and return to the parking lot.

George Miller

George Miller Regional Shoreline at Point Richmond near the Richmond-San Rafael Bridge is a little stretch of bay shore with fishing from rip-rap boulders and a small sandy beach, a grassy hill to climb, and picnic areas. Follow route 17 through Richmond, turn left from Standard Ave. onto Garrard, and go through the tunnel to the park, or take AC Transit bus #72 to the end of Standard Ave. and walk through the tunnel.

Point Isabel

Point Isabel Regional Shoreline is a short stretch of filled shoreline next to the U.S. Postal Service Bulk Mail Center in Richmond. It offers fishing, bicycle path, turf area, picnicking. Go west from I-80 on Central Ave.

Port View Park

A most interesting small park in Oakland will be found at the very end of Seventh Street, the western tip of the port of Oakland. There is lawn and picnic tables, a short fishing pier, and a tower several stories high which you can walk up and enjoy a view of the busy harbor and the San Francisco Skyline surprisingly near across the bay.

Lake Merritt

Unlike most of the places described in this book, Lake Merritt shows very little of the wild natural environment. It is a man-made landscape right in the middle of Oakland, surrounded by high-rise offices and apartments. But its urban character gives it much of its appeal as an oasis of green grass and trees and blue sparkling water before a backdrop of big city skyline.

This saltwater tidal lake was created early in Oakland's history by a low dam across a marshy slough. It is circled by a three mile trail along the city park shoreline which is very popular with runners and strollers. Along the way are Children's Fairyland, a boathouse and a small bird sanctuary, the nation's first wildlife refuge.

The lake is easily accessible from BART—three blocks east from the 19th Street Station, or the same distance north from the Lake Merritt Station.

While in the neighborhood, don't pass up an opportunity to look through the Oakland Museum, 10th and Oak Streets, the best exhibits you'll find anywhere of California ecology, history, and art.

Crown Beach

Robert W. Crown Memorial State Beach in Alameda, operated by the EBRPD, is a 2½ mile stretch of bay shore beach well suited to beachcombers, joggers, fishermen, birdwatchers and sand castle architects. In the last century the site of Neptune Beach, a large amusement park with roller coaster, etc., it now has a much quieter atmosphere, with picnic tables, swimming and wading, and naturalist programs.

To get there, take the Alameda exit from Freeway 17, go through the tube and continue on Webster St., turning left on Central Ave., right on 8th St. AC Transit bus #63 will take you there too.

San Leandro Bay

San Leandro Bay Regional Shoreline is a strip of bay fill and salt marsh around most of this shallow arm of San Francisco Bay which is almost enclosed by Alameda, Bay Farm Island (where the Oakland Airport is), and industrial Oakland. A trail follows most of the shore giving close-up views of the salt marsh and its inhabitants, open water and numerous shorebirds, fishermen, and sometimes noisy presence of nearby factories.

A small city playground and park, Bay Park Refuge, is one convenient access point. Take the Nimitz Freeway (17) south to 66th Ave., go south on the frontage road, Oakport St., right on Hassler, right on Edgewater. The trail may also be reached from Hegenberger Road, and a couple of parking areas on Doolittle Drive north of the airport provide access to the recently developed west shore. AC Transit bus #57 from the Coliseum BART Station will take you to the trails ending on Hegenberger Rd.

San Leandro Shoreline

Next to the San Leandro Marina there is a nice park with spacious green grass, playgrounds and picnic areas. A trail out on a little peninsula from the park is a nice place for walking or running and it has a parcourse set-up for additional exercise. It is also permissible to follow the shoreline for several miles south from here, though the "super sewer" construction just beyond the park doesn't make it too inviting.

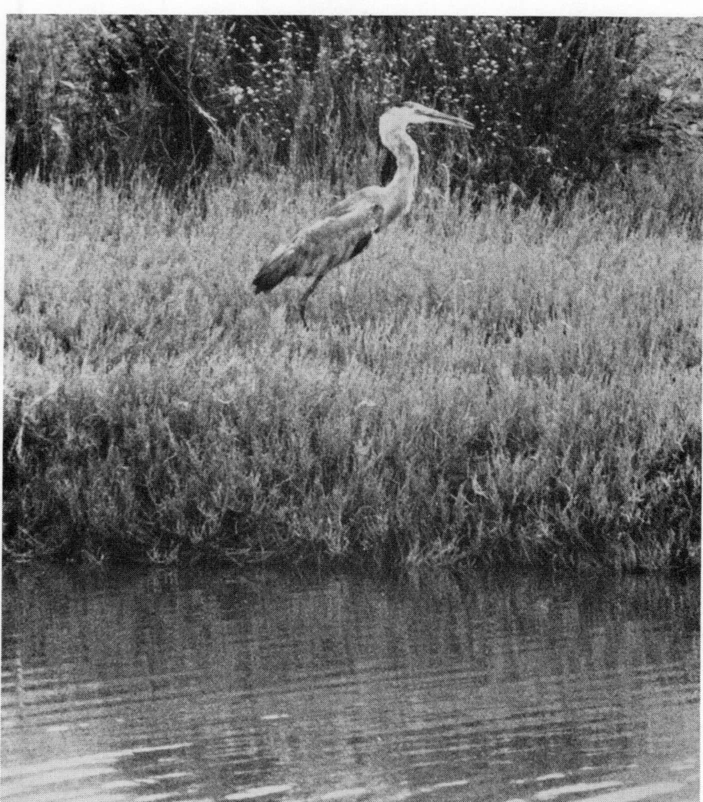

Great Blue Heron, San Leandro Bay

Hayward Shoreline

Hayward Shoreline

A large area of bay shore in Hayward is now in public ownership and will soon be developed for public access. Right now it is officially closed, but hiking into the area from the end of Winton Avenue is not really discouraged. This area was planned for open space use and parts of it acquired through a cooperative effort of the City of Hayward, Hayward Area Recreation District (HARD), and the EBRPD. An interesting feature of the shoreline is that a large area of former salt ponds has been re-connected with the bay so that its tidal action will allow the area to return to its original condition as salt marsh. This is the largest project of this type on the bay shore, and it will be interesting to see how well the marsh will restore itself.

Alameda Creek Trail *12 mi. one way/level*

This long trail follows Alameda Creek and its Flood Control Channel for twelve miles, from the mouth of Niles Canyon through Fremont and Union City, past Coyote Hills to the bay. It is actually two parallel trails, one for horses on the north side and one for bicycles on the south side. Both sides may be used by pedestrians.

This was the first regional trail created by the EBRPD, which brought to reality a new concept in trails—those which leave the parks to connect with other parks, transit connections, and population centers, giving us many new opportunities for recreation and transportation using muscle power rather than gas. Planning is currently underway to extend the trail east through Niles Canyon to the town of Sunol.

The trail may be reached from several parking areas along the way: 1) Old Canyon Rd. just east of Niles Canyon Rd. and Mission Blvd., 2) Jamieson Quarry off of Paseo Padre Parkway, 3) Decoto Rd., 4) Beard Rd., 5) Hop Ranch Rd. off Alvarado Niles Rd., and 6) Newark Blvd. AC Transit bus #26 serves the eastern end of the trail and #21 & 29 cross the trail on Decoto Rd. All three lines stop at the Union City and the Fremont BART stations.

Near the eastern end of the trail, the regional park district owns several ponds in old gravel pits, which will be developed as a park in the future. At present, one of them, Shinn Pond, is open to the public.

Coyote Hills

Coyote Hills Regional Park is an interesting and unusual place. There are marshes of cattails, graceful long necked birds standing in shallow water, and Indian shellmounds. There is a miniature range of hills with multicolored rocks jutting out from their rounded slopes. There are the shores of a vast network of salt evaporation ponds and wide open views of the bay. This park is an excellent place for bird-watching. It is also a great place for bicycles, with a long, nearly level, paved trail for their use.

Two thousand years of Indian history is found in the four shell mounds in the park. The Ohlone Indians ate shellfish and discarded the shells on the mounds. Their dead were also buried there. They lived near these mounds up until about 1800. A recent book which I heartily recommend, Malcolm Margolin's *The Ohlone Way,* tells the fascinating story of everyday life in an Indian village like one that stood here in Coyote Hills. I would also recommend a tour of a shell mound with a park naturalist for a look at the excavation of the mound and a very interesting talk. Programs are given there every weekend during good weather. Call 471-4967 for information.

To get to the park, take Freeway 17 to Fremont, go right on Jarvis Ave., right on Newark Blvd., left on Patterson Ranch Rd. and proceed into the park to the visitor center.

Short Walks

Red Hill, the highest in the park (291 feet) can be easily climbed by heading left from the west end of the visitor center parking lot. Go a few yards, then leave the road to the right and climb past picnic tables and pine trees, turning right at a saddle, and up the hill. Look out across the big ponds and dikes of the salt evaporators and the open waters of the bay. Note the colorful outcrops of Franciscan rock. Descend the far side, turn right, and follow the road back to the visitor center, a walk of a little more than a mile.

For me, the marshes are the most fascinating part of this park. Only a few steps from the visitor center out onto a boardwalk takes you into

Freshwater marsh

a world of cattails, still waters and birds, a world quietly teeming with life. Early in the morning it is especially peaceful and in the open water there may be flocks of ducks and coots and maybe a few big white egrets.

Chochenyo Trail *2.1 mi./level*

This route circles the freshwater marsh area and passes a couple of shell mounds (no bicycles or dogs). From the visitor center follow the dirt road lined with cattails just left of the boardwalk. Turn right on the Chochenyo Trail and watch the birds as you pass a large pond. Bear to the right and pass a shell mound (fenced—to see inside take naturalist tour). Continue across damp fields, then at the park entrance, turn right on a bicycle trail which parallels the road back to the visitor center.

Bicycle Trail *3.3 mi./100 ft. climb*

This trail, perfect for bicycles, but also used by hikers, winds around the base of the hills along the shores of the salt ponds and beside the marshes.

From the visitor center, follow the trail beside the entrance road back a quarter mile, cross the road and go through the other parking lot. Continue on the bicycle trail around a marshy area, over a low gap in the hills and northwest along the shore. Round the north end of the hills where a connection with the Alameda Creek Trail branches left, going east and west along the flood control channel. Return along the east side of the hills to the visitor center.

Into the Wildlife Refuge *3.4 mi./level*

This route leads out along the dikes of the salt evaporators into the San Francisco Bay National Wildlife Refuge (see next page). You'll see salt marsh life and lots of birds, but what impresses me most about this area is the feeling of vast open spaces, big sky, calm water and not much else. From the Coyote Hills Visitor Center go right from the west end of the parking lot and follow the bicycle trail to the north end of the hills. Just past the Alameda Creek Trail connection, there is a wooden deck and a trail down the hill. Go right on that trail, into the Wildlife Refuge and out on a dike beside the salt ponds. Wind around and come to the Alameda Creek Trail. To the left, this paved trail follows the flood control channel another 1.6 miles to its outlet into the bay. Unless you want to make this side trip, turn right and follow the Alameda Creek Trail back to the northern tip of the hills and return to the visitor center on the bicycle trail.

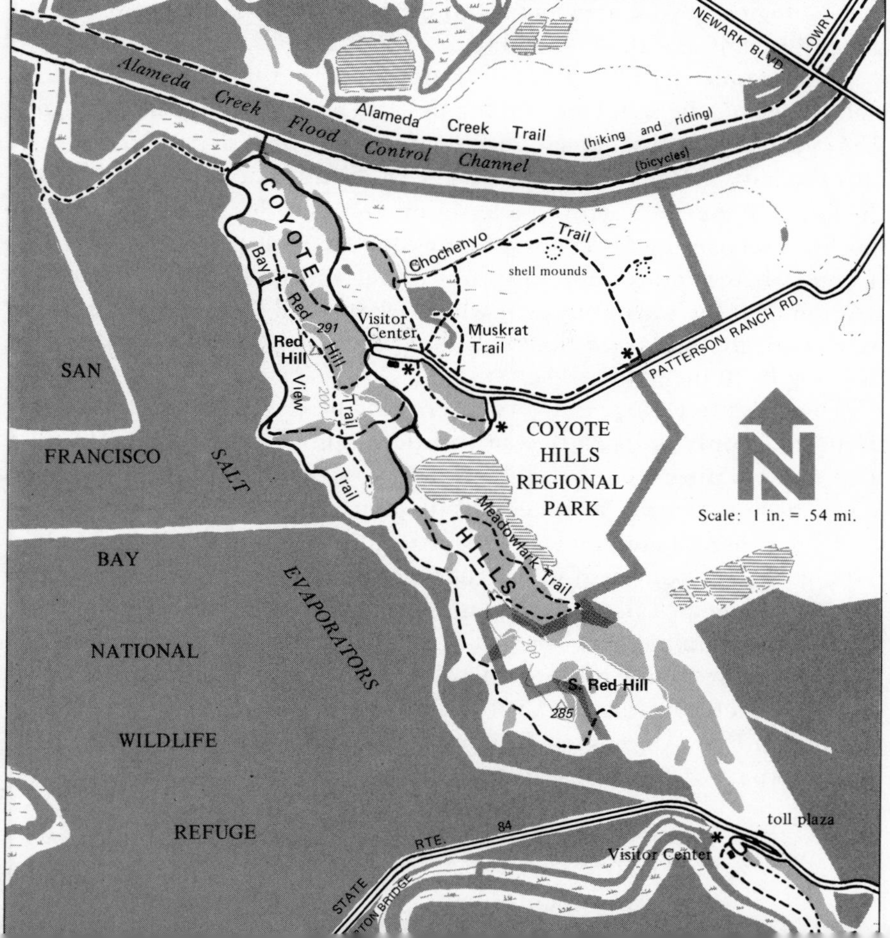

S. F. Bay National Wildlife Refuge

A majority of the ducks and other birds which migrate in the Pacific Flyway depend on a stopover in the extensive wetlands of the South Bay. Harbor seals also depend on this area as a breeding ground. Countless smaller animals call this area home. This broad expanse of salt ponds, marshes, levees and sloughs recently came under the protection of the Department of the Interior, U.S. Fish and Wildlife Service, saving this ecologically vital area and its wildlife for its own sake as well as for the enjoyment and understanding of us humans.

In September, 1979, only a few months after the refuge was officially opened, the San Jose and Santa Clara sewage treatment plan in Alviso accidently discharged huge quantities of partially treated sewage into the bay, killing all of the fish and wildlife south of the Dumbarton Bridge. It happened again to a lesser extent in 1980. The animal life has been recovering faster than first expected, and there is plenty to see if you visit the refuge, but let us not forget this unfortunate demonstration that the technology on which we depend for our everyday lives is not infallible and that we should do all we can to keep this kind of thing from happening again.

The Wildlife Refuge is a very interesting place to look around, though it is only in its early stages of development at this time. In the future, the Visitor Center will be fixed up with permanent displays and many more trails will be opened leading out into the wetlands.

To get there, take Freeway 17 south to Fremont, get off on Jarvis Ave., go right a couple of miles, then right on Thornton Ave. and left into the refuge just before the Dumbarton Bridge Toll Plaza.

One short trail is now open from the Visitor Center. Follow the dirt road south over a low hill providing spacious views. Make a sharp right and head back towards the Visitor Center a few feet above salt marsh and slough often populated by many shorebirds. Another trail in the northern part of the refuge is described on the preceding page.

2. Berkeley Hills

East Bay Skyline Trail

The East Bay Skyline National Recreational Trail is a 30 mile riding and hiking trail along the crest of the East Bay hills from Richmond to Castro Valley, 30 miles of woods and grassland, ridgetops and canyons, often seeming quite remote though never more than a few miles from the city.

This was the first trail to be designated as a National Recreational Trail under the National Trails System Act of 1968. At first (1970) it was just 15 miles of existing trail in Redwood and Chabot parks. Through purchases of private property, aided by federal Land and Water Conservation funds, and by licenses with public agencies, the trail was extended to its present length in 1979.

It is a long way to hike or even ride in one day (though possible) so that most people will enjoy the trail a section at a time—which is not hard to do because there are many points of access along the way, some served by public transportation.

In order to keep all the trails of each area together in the same part of the book, each section of the Skyline Trail will be described with the parks that it goes through or near.

Wildcat Canyon .... p. 43
Tilden .... p. 49
Sibley and Huckleberry .... p. 54
Redwood .... p. 63
Chabot .... p. 69

Wildcat Canyon

Wildcat Canyon Regional Park is an area of rounded grassy hills, wooded arroyos, grazing cattle and beautiful little Wildcat Creek which flows in its shaded rocky bed nearly year round. It is a place of quiet, of space, a place to appreciate the beautiful ordinariness of earth and sky. It is an uncrowded park, because it is minimally developed and not too widely known, in contrast to Tilden Park which adjoins it to the southeast.

To get there, take I-80 north to Richmond, exit at Amador St.-Solano Ave., continue on the frontage road, Amador St., turn right on McBryde Ave., go several blocks, and come to an intersection opposite the stone gated entrance to Alvarado Park. Go straight through onto Park Ave., then straight as Park turns right. At the end of the road there is a parking lot.

The park may also be entered from the end of Clark Road south off San Pablo Dam Rd. in El Sobrante, ¼ mile from AC Transit bus #69B.

AC Transit buses #7 or 70 stop at Arlington and Rifle Range Rd. which you can follow to its end at the park entrance and walk down a trail to meet the Wildcat Creek Trail (1 mi.).

Havey Canyon Trail

Mezue & Havey Canyon Trails *5.2 mi./700 ft. climb*

This route follows the creek a ways, then climbs to the top of San Pablo Ridge with lots of open space and good views, then comes back down through a pretty little canyon—a thoroughly enjoyable walk.

Follow the gravel road from the parking lot, the Wildcat Creek Trail, as it heads up the valley. To the right, down by the creek, are several picnic areas. After walking not quite a mile, make a sharp left turn onto a dirt road heading back up the hillside, the Mezue (mez-way) Trail. Climb the shoulder of a hill and arrive panting at the top of the ridge. From a nearby hilltop, you can see all of San Pablo Bay from San Francisco to Carquinez Straits. The Clark-Boas Trail branches left along the ridge. Go right (south) on Nimitz Way which becomes a paved road around the next hill. Just before the power lines, turn right on a dirt road traversing down across the hill, the Havey Canyon Trail. Pass several big eucyalptus trees, long ago the site of the Havey family's ranch house, and follow a tiny creek through willows and vine thickets, bay trees and mossy rocks. Turn right on the Wildcat Creek Trail, complete the loop and return to the parking lot.

Skyline Trail—Wildcat Canyon

4.1 mi./700 ft. climb southbound, downhill northbound

The 30 mile East Bay Skyline National Recreational Trail begins here in Wildcat Canyon. This section of the trail goes up Wildcat Creek, climbs a little canyon and continues southeast along San Pablo Ridge to Tilden Park. On the ridge there are good views all around.

From the parking lot, follow the same route as the above, but in reverse direction, going up the Wildcat Creek Trail, left on the Havey Canyon Trail, to the ridgetop. Leave the above route by turning right on Nimitz Way, a paved road, and enjoy expansive views. Follow the widely rounded crest of the ridge, the site of a 1950's missile base, south to the boundary of Tilden Park. Along the way, the Eagle's Nest Trail branches left and descends a couple of miles to San Pablo Reservoir (permit required, see p. 131). For the next section, see p. 49.

Wildcat Creek Trail

3.3 mi./200 ft. climb southbound, downhill northbound

This is an easy trail through gentle countryside. Follow the Wildcat Creek Trail all the way from the parking lot, gradually climbing up the valley, entering Tilden Nature Area (no dogs), passing Jewel Lake, and ending up at the Environmental Education Center. Walk back or have someone meet you there. AC Transit bus #67 stops ½ mile up Canon Dr.

Clark-Boas Trail

2.1 mi./1000 ft. climb southbound, 200 ft. northbound

From the Clark Road entrance to the park, south off San Pablo Dam Rd. in El Sobrante, follow a dirt road up the hill, past fields of thistles and a small cypress grove to the top of San Pablo Ridge near its northern end. Go left, then right, climbing steeply up the crest and continuing up and down along the top of the ridge, with extensive views, a couple of miles to Nimitz Way and the Mezue Trail.

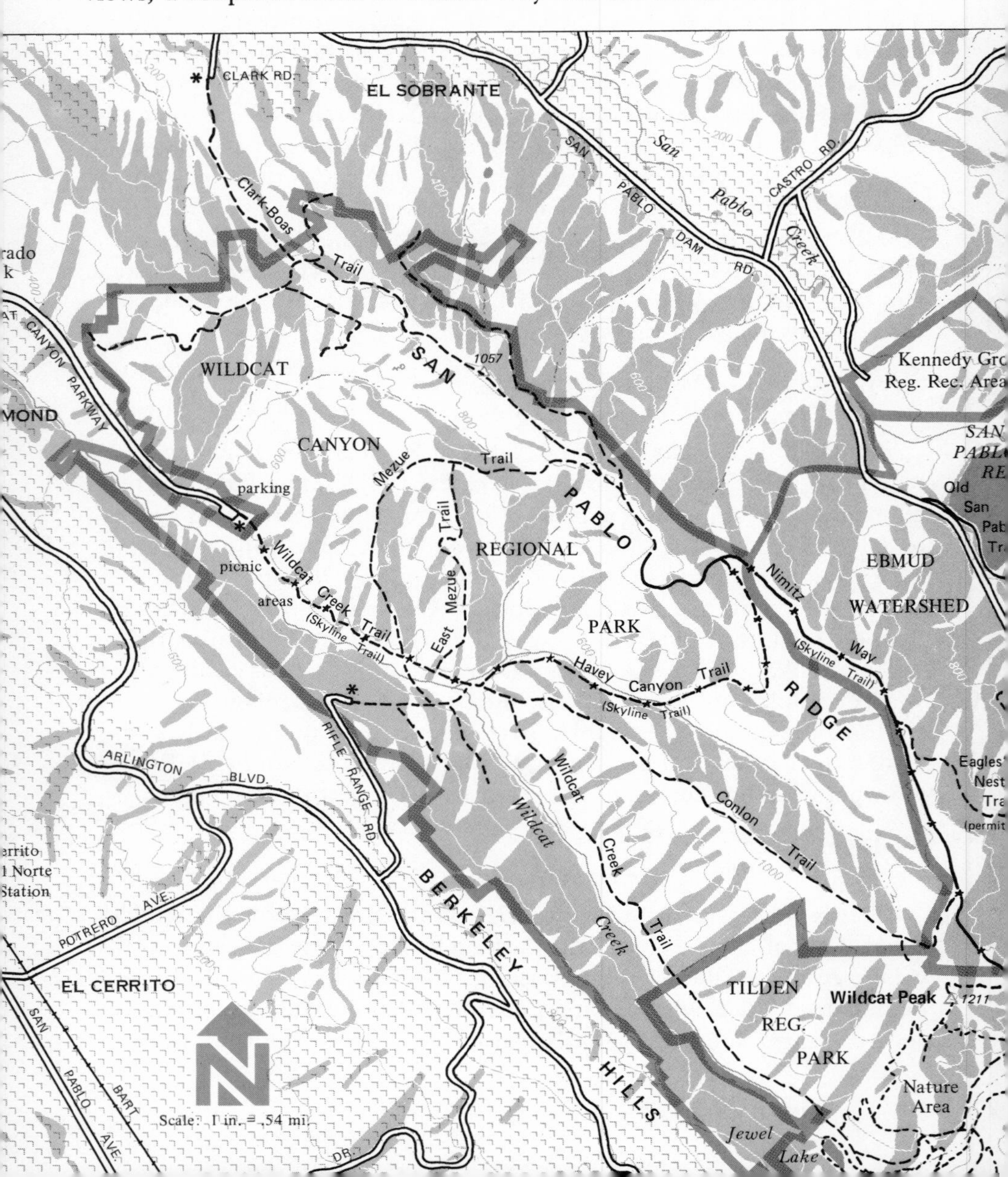

Tilden

Charles Lee Tilden Regional Park— the sounds of merry-go-round music, radios, laughing and splashing at the lake, barbeque smoke drifting through old eucalpytus trees; sitting on a rock in the sun contemplating the rolling hills of grass and brush or jogging in blowing fog on a high ridge.

Tilden is one of the most popular, the oldest, and best developed of the parks in the area. On warm summer days it may be mobbed with people, especially at the Lake Anza swimming area. But on winter week-days you may have the park to yourself. There are facilities for tennis and golf, ball fields, an antique merry-go-round, a small steam train ride, pony rides, riding stables near the park, and a nature area with a little farm with young animals for the kids to enjoy. It also has some good trails for hiking, cycling or riding, and some interesting natural areas despite all the development.

The park is situated in the upper valley of Wildcat Creek, which flows northwest through Wildcat Canyon Park to the bay. The valley is bounded on the west by a wooded ridge over which spill the residential areas of Berkeley and Kensington, and on the east by higher grassy San Pablo Ridge. Unusual outcrops of volcanic rock add an interesting touch to the landscape. Large areas of the park have in recent years seen great changes, where frost-killed eucalyptus forest has been clear-cut. The resulting rutted weedy hillsides are mostly on the west slope and are not encountered on most of the following trails.

There are a number of ways to reach the park, as follows:

1) From Berkeley: North on Shattuck, right on Hearst, then:
    a) Left on Spruce, which winds up the hill to the Spruce Gate.
    b) Left on Euclid, right on Rose, left on Tamalpais, right on Shasta, which winds up to the Shasta Gate.
    c) Right on Gayley, left on Rimway, left on Centennial Dr., up Strawberry Canyon to the Golf Gate.
2) From Freeway 24 follow Claremont Ave. all the way up the canyon, turn left on Grizzly Peak Blvd., then right at the South Gate.
3) Take Freeway 24 to Orinda, turn left on Camino Pablo, then left on Wildcat Canyon Rd., entering the park at Inspiration Point.

AC Transit bus #67 stops near the Spruce Gate, ½ mile from the Nature Area entrance or the starting point for the trail along Wildcat Creek. Bus #7 goes along Grizzly Peak Blvd. providing access to the Shasta Gate, and stops near the Golf Gate.

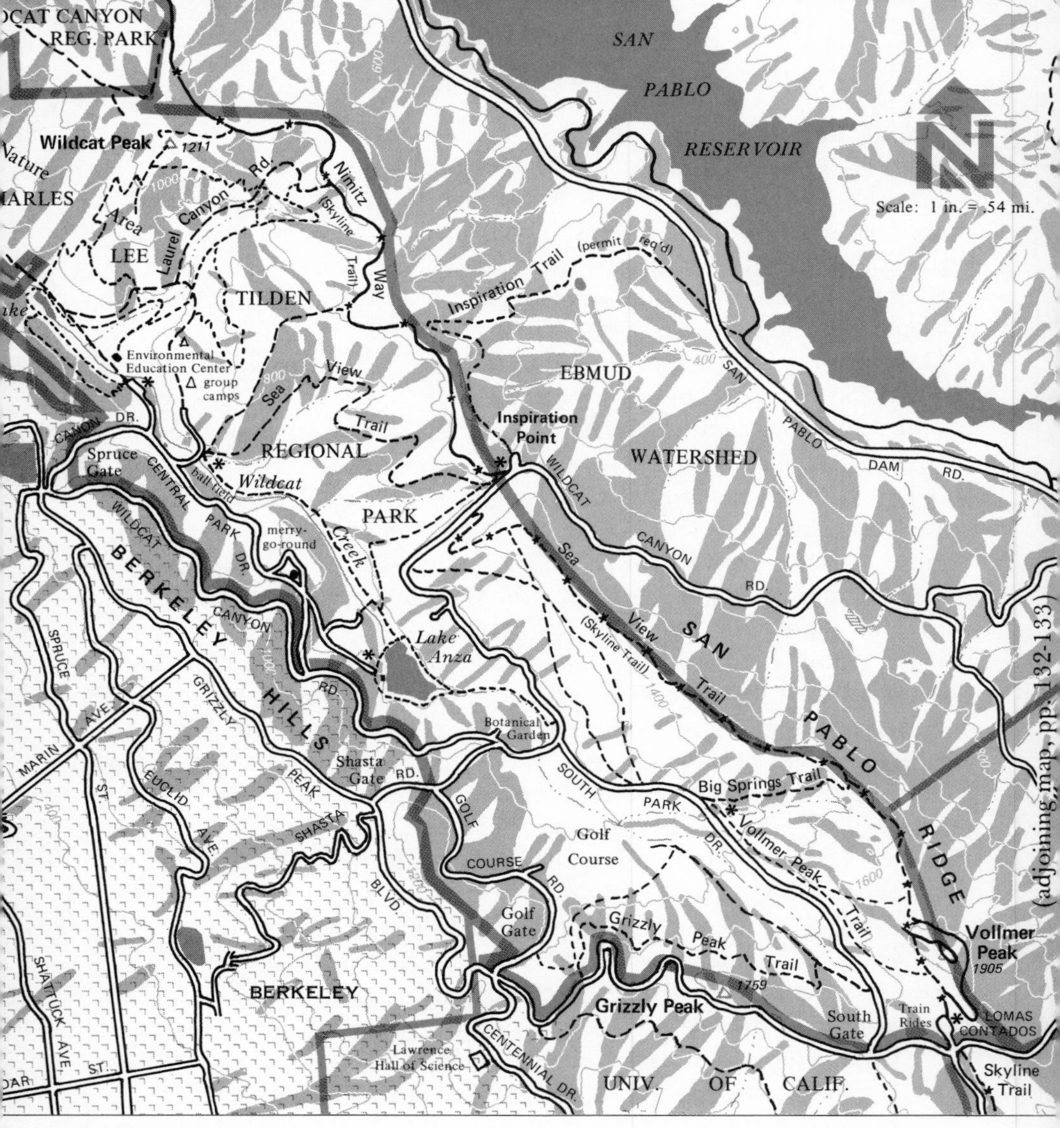

Nature Area

This is the most natural part of Tilden, and has the most interesting and scenic trails. The following two walks are in this area. Follow Central Park Drive past the merry-go-round and tennis courts to its end at the Nature Area parking lot (or Canon Dr. down from the Spruce Gate, then left). While in the Nature Area, follow the rules: disturbing or removing any plant or animal life is forbidden and no dogs are allowed.

Just inside the front gate is the Environmental Education Center, which has ecology exhibits for school kids, and the naturalists there lead tours and can tell you all about the living things of the area.

Sunset, Golden Gate, from Wildcat Peak

Nimitz Way

Cliff and caves, below Lake Anza

Jewel Lake Trail *1.2 mi./level*

This is an easy, pleasant walk which passes many interesting natural features which are pointed out in the guide book which you may borrow. The trail starts just behind the Environmental Education Center. Follow the posts with the blue ducks (🦆), winding through woods and fields, across a road, and through a damp area of willows, rushes and frogs, on a raised walkway, coming out on the shore of Jewel Lake. Watch the ducks out on this small weedy pond. Continue around the lake, and into dense vine thickets, then ferns and big bay trees with gnarled trunks, and end up at the parking lot.

Laurel Canyon & Wildcat Peak *3.0 mi./800 ft. climb*

This route is longer and more strenuous than the Jewel Lake Trail, and it climbs through woods and fields to Wildcat Peak, which offers an excellent view of the area.

The trail starts just left of the little farm. Follow the posts with a laurel (bay) leaf (🍃). Climb gently through eucalyptus forest. Cross a road and continue. A few yards down this road to the right, the Pine Tree Trail (🌲) starts. It climbs through a grove of Monterey pines, then brush, and finally descends to rejoin the Laurel Canyon Trail, which meanwhile has gone through brush and woods, still gently climbing. A trail branches left and crosses the creek to Laurel Canyon Road. Climb a little more, cross the creekbed, and turn left at a fork. Descend through coyote brush and sage brush, willows, elderberries and horsetails. Turn right beginning the Wildcat Peak Trail (⛰), and switchback up the grassy hillside, crossing the Laurel Canyon Road, and climbing steeply up the flanks of Wildcat Peak. Turn right on another trail and climb to the top. The view is a panorama of much of the Bay Area, from Oakland and San Francisco through Marin and Sonoma Counties.

Descend the way you came up the last hundred yards, then go straight ahead down the ridge. Watch for a signpost and follow its arrow to the right. Switchback down through brush, then blackberry thickets and woods, and into eucalyptus. Turn left on the Sylvan Trail (🌿) (the Wildcat Peak Trail continues right, switchbacking down beside a wooded ravine to Jewel Lake). Walk through the eucalyptus, cross Laurel Canyon Road, and follow the Jewel Lake Trail a short distance back to the Environmental Education Center.

Along Wildcat Creek *1.6 mi. one way/400 ft. climb*

This route follows the creek from the ball field near the tennis courts, up past Lake Anza to the botanical gardens. It is an easy and interesting walk.

Just across the creek from the parking area by the field, two trails start on the right: the wide Sea View Trail to the left, and the creek trail to the right. Follow the latter across a tiny creek, across a field, and into the woods beside a small cascade. Continue along the shady creek bank. On the far side is a curious rock formation—a 100 ft. cliff riddled with caves. The top of this promontory can be reached by a short steep path from the merry-go-round. Just beyond, a road and picnic areas are close by across the creek, and a trail branches left which climbs to Inspiration Point, making possible a loop via the Sea View Trail or Nimitz Way and Laurel Canyon Road. The trail becomes narrow and indistinct as it passes a small stone building and climbs the dam to Lake Anza. Continue around the left shore past people sunning on the rocks. Stay on the left side of the creek at the inlet, where a trail branches to the right across a bridge and circling the lake. The creek is especially pretty above here, splashing over old worn rock, through green and shady redwoods. About ¼ mile above the lake, the trail is blocked by a fence. Climb the bank to the left along the fence to the paved road, and follow it a short distance to the right to the botanical gardens. It would be well worth your time to walk through the gardens, which contain a wide variety of native California plants. This is an excellent place to identify plants you may have seen on the trails. Return by the same route.

Skyline Trail—Nimitz Way

1.9 mi./100 ft. climb southbound, 100 ft. northbound

From the southern boundary of Wildcat Canyon Regional Park, the Skyline Trail continues along San Pablo Ridge on Nimitz Way, passing Wildcat Peak which is nearby on the right, and gently winding along the grassy ridge down to Wildcat Canyon Road at Inspiration Point.

Nimitz Way is an excellent place for bicycles. It is a paved road, closed to motor vehicles, that winds along the hills for three miles with no steep climbs and with room for hikers, joggers and horses too. To enjoy this section of trail without coming all the way from Wildcat Canyon, start from Inspiration Point and follow the road north.

Skyline Trail—Sea View Trail

2.8 mi./900 ft. climb southbound, 300 ft. northbound

The Sea View Trail is a dirt road which follows the crest of San Pablo Ridge to Vollmer Peak, the highest point in the Berkeley Hills. This is the only trail in Tilden where dogs are permitted to run unleashed. The views are impressive.

From Inspiration Point, follow Wildcat Canyon Road a few hundred yards to the right until the Sea View Trail leaves the road on the left, a wide dirt road with a bar across it. Climb a couple of switchbacks through eucalyptus to the ridge crest, gradually ascend through a series of little pine groves, then steeply to a high point of the ridge with a wide open view—a good spot for a summer afternoon, watching the fog as it pours in stopped motion through the Golden Gate, the bay silvery in the sun. Descend to a saddle, where the Big Springs Trail branches right. Climb again along the ridge and near the top turn right on a paved road, then right on a trail (or continue on the road to the top of Vollmer Peak, a worthwhile side trip). Descend to the intersection of Grizzly Peak Blvd. and Lomas Contados, the steam train rides, and parking lot. For the next section of the Skyline Trail, see p. 54.

Kennedy Grove

Kennedy Grove Regional Recreation Area is a small park with picnic areas and lawn, just below San Pablo Dam in El Sobrante, which is presently only available for use by groups with reservations (223-7840).

Strawberry Canyon

In 1866, Frederick Law Olmstead was hired to provide a design for the new College of California and the neighboring village of Berkeley. That design included the provision that Strawberry Canyon be set aside as a scenic preserve. That is why it is today one of the few unspoiled areas on the west slope of the Berkeley Hills. The land is owned by the University of California, and signs all over the area proclaim it an "Ecological Study Area," which means it is under generally the same restrictions as the regional parks.

The canyon displays a wide variety of plant and animal life, including a dozen or so different species of conifers, most of which are introduced, but appear right at home with the natives. The canyon is not all unspoiled wilderness however; the north side is covered with the buildings of the Lawrence Berkeley Laboratories. At the mouth of the canyon is the Memorial Stadium, and above that is the student-faculty swimming pool. Of special interest are the botanical gardens further up the canyon. Nicely landscaped paths lead through countless beautiful and unusual plants from all over the world. There is also a large area devoted to native California plants.

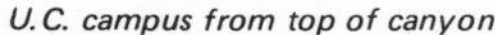

U.C. campus from top of canyon

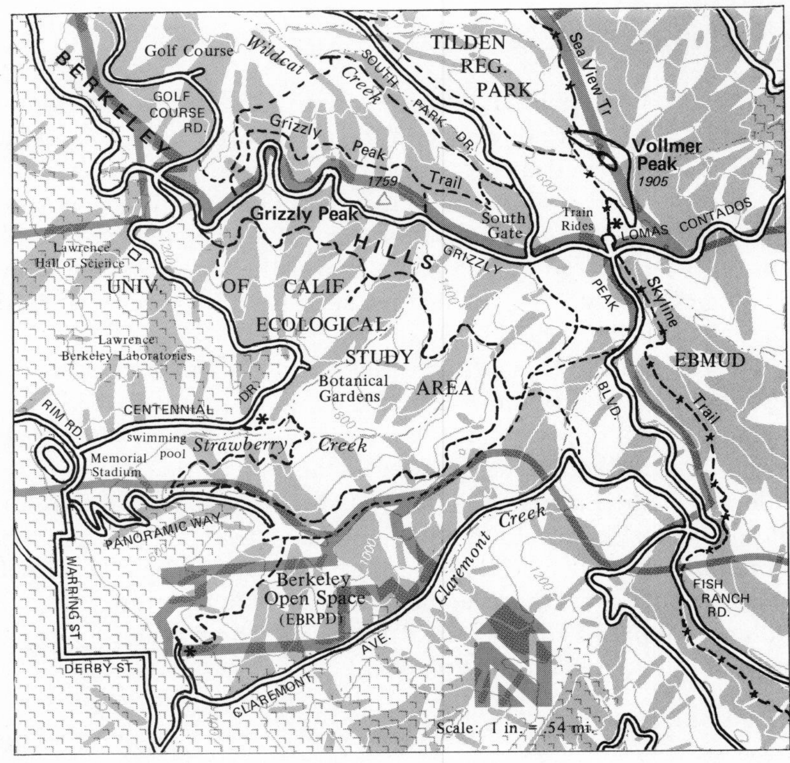

To get there from University Ave. in Berkeley, follow that street until it ends at the campus, turn left on Oxford, right on Hearst, right on Gayley, left on Rimway, then left on Centennial Dr., which leads up the canyon to the starting point for the route below, a small parking area about ½ mile beyond the swimming pool.

Grizzly Peak Loop *8.0 mi./1200 ft. climb*

This route climbs up out of the canyon and circles Grizzly Peak, part of the trail being in Tilden Park. It offers an interesting sampling of Berkeley Hills ecology as well as many good views. Take note that this trail is easily accessible via BART and the shuttlebus "Humphery-Go-Bart" which runs up to the Lawrence Hall of Science on weekdays—making possible a one-way walk to (or down from) that point with a ride back.

Start from a small parking area below the botanical gardens. Up the road a few feet, a dirt road begins on the right; follow it through big oak and bay trees, brush, vines and ferns, crossing three small creeks that join below as Strawberry Creek. Gradually climb up the south slope of the canyon, passing small groves of redwoods, pines, firs and cypress. At the top of a ridge, come upon houses and a city street. Go around the fence on your left just before reaching the street, and climb up the ridge. Soon reach and go left on another dirt road along the hillside. Pass several more groves of conifers, then go through coyote bush and poison oak. Climb gradually, traversing just below the ridge-top. A couple of roads branch right (you will complete the loop on the second). Contour around the head of the canyon, passing shady ravines, grassy, rocky hillsides, and logged eucalyptus forest. Come upon a large research building and Grizzly Peak Blvd. (go left on the road to reach the shuttlebus stop at Lawrence Hall of Science). Turn right and follow the road about 100 yards. Follow a rough trail left, down the hill a short way, and turn right on a trail contouring the hillside. A few yards below, a parallel trail descends above the golf course to South Park Drive. The upper trail, the Grizzly Peak Trail, gradually climbs, getting into dense brush and vines. It is easy walking, but watch out for poison oak. Almost under the power lines, cross another trail. Soon descend, turn right on a dirt road, go about ¼ mile to South Park Drive, turn right and follow the road up to the South Gate. Cross Grizzly Peak Blvd., and go straight over the slight hill covered with sprouting eucalyptus stumps. Cross a trail, go over another small hill, and down the pine forested ridge separating Strawberry and Claremont Canyons. Come out of the woods on a grassy hillside with good views of the campus, the bay, and the City. Turn right on a dirt road, then left, completing the loop, and retrace your route down into the canyon.

Lake Temescal

This small reservoir, the East Bay's oldest, built in 1869, has a nice beach for swimming in the summertime, picnicking, fishing, and a pleasant little trail around the lake. Take the Broadway-Highway 13 exit from Freeway 24 or enter from Broadway Terrace just west of Highway 13. AC Transit bus #59 goes by the latter entrance.

Sibley & Huckleberry

Sibley Regional Preserve and Huckleberry Botanic Preserve are undeveloped parklands in the Berkeley Hills above Oakland through which passes the East Bay Skyline Trail.

Sibley Preserve used to be named Round Top after the 1763 ft. peak in the center of the park. The slopes of the peak were largely covered with eucalyptus trees several years ago, but they were hard hit by the freeze of 1972 and most of them have been cleared leaving stumps and sprouts. Near the top there is a nice grove of Monterey pines. Millions of years ago Roundtop was a volcano, a caldera full of bubbling lava and mud. All that is left of it now is this big bump of volcanic rock. About a quarter mile north of the peak, on a dug-up ridge that used to be a quarry of Kaiser Sand and Gravel, there is another volcanic vent, this one cut away so that the path of the lava can be traced. The park district is considering making a trail through this area to show off its interesting geological features.

A visit to Huckleberry Botanic Preserve is a must for anyone interested in native plants. It has a unique flora, including huckleberry, golden chinquapin, several manzanitas and a wide variety of other plants mixed into broadleaf evergreen woods. Even if you aren't botanically inclined, it's a lovely place to walk.

To get to Sibley, take Freeway 24 east, get off at the last exit before the tunnel, double back and cross the freeway, turn left, then right on Tunnel Rd., which becomes Skyline Blvd. near the top of the hills. Stay right at the intersection of Grizzly Peak Blvd. and the entrance to the preserve is on the left, with limited parking. The entrance to Huckleberry, with a small parking area, is just .4 miles further south on Skyline Blvd. AC Transit bus #18 going up Snake Rd. stops within ½ mi. of Huckleberry and not quite a mile from Sibley.

Skyline Trail—Tilden to Sibley

3.2 mi./400 ft. climb southbound, 700 ft. northbound

After leaving Tilden Park, the Skyline Trail is a relatively new trail passing through watershed and private land, dipping down along the east slope of the hills above the Caldecott Tunnel and climbing to the shoulder of Round Top in Sibley Regional Preserve.

From the parking lot for the train rides in Tilden, cross Lomas Contados at its intersection with Grizzly Peak Blvd. and go through the gate almost hidden in brush below the road. The trail contours the hillside below Grizzly Peak Blvd. through coyote bush, poison oak and live oaks, then weedy grassland and low brush below a microwave tower. Enjoy sweeping views of Mt. Diablo and surrounding hills. Descend, cross Fish Ranch Road, and continue across the hillside with the busy freeway (state hwy. 24) disappearing into the tunnel below, seeming far removed from the wild environment of the trail. Cross a paved road coming up from the tunnel, and gently climb up the valley towards Round Top, the high wooded peak to the south. Keep to the

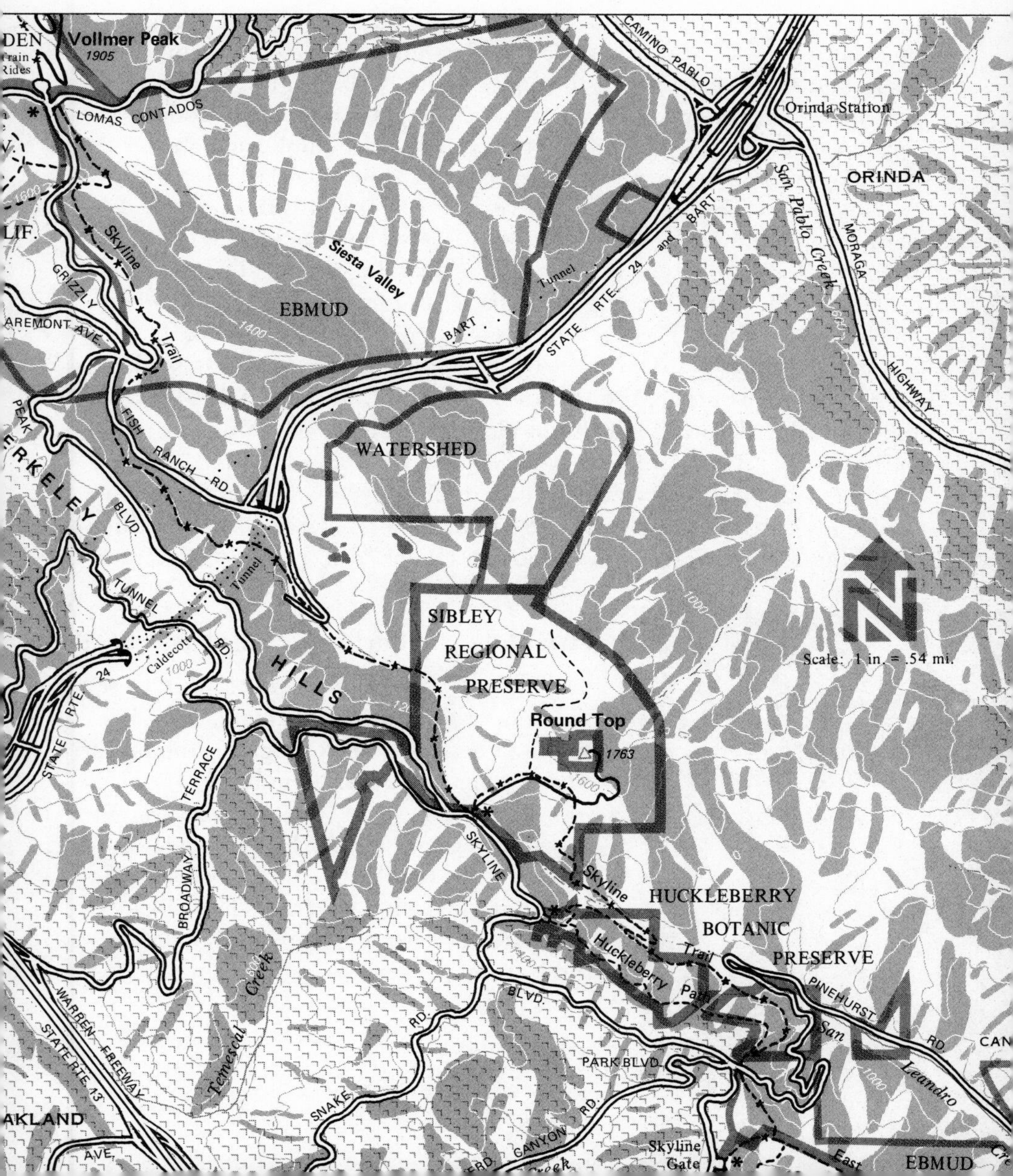

right and climb through woods and brush with views of the barren gravel quarries on the neighboring ridge and arrive at the entrance to Sibley Regional Preserve on Skyline Blvd.

Skyline Trail—Sibley to Redwood

2.6 mi./600 ft. climb southbound, 700 ft. northbound

A few feet to the east on the paved service road at the entrance to Sibley Regional Preserve, just before the gate, follow a path to the left, the Skyline Trail, through Monterey pines and over the shoulder of Round Top. Cross the service road leading to the antennae on the peak, and switchback down through coyote bush into the canyon. Cross the headwaters of San Leandro Creek, climb up the wooded opposite bank and turn left (the trail to the right climbs up to the entrance to the Huckleberry Preserve on Skyline Blvd.).

Now in the Huckleberry Preserve, contour the hillside, steep and densely wooded with bay and madrone, ferns and huckleberries. This beautiful section of trail was the last part of the Skyline Trail to be built and it held up its completion for a couple of years with condemnation proceedings. You may thank the perseverence of the park district and much hard work of volunteer trail builders as you walk here. After a long mile, the Huckleberry Path branches back to the right and the Skyline Trail climbs along the hillside and crosses Pinehurst Road at its intersection with Skyline Blvd. Find the trail angling to the left (east) side of the ridge and follow it around the hill, turn right on the wide East Ridge Trail and soon arrive at the parking lot at the Skyline Gate of Redwood Regional Park. Next section, p. 63.

Huckleberry Path *2.2 mi./400 ft. climb*

This narrow path is the best place to see the unique flora of the preserve. It is also simply a beautiful walk. Begin at the preserve entrance near 7090 Skyline Blvd., and contour southeast for a mile or so through dense woods and brush. To make a loop out of this walk, turn left on the Skyline Trail and contour back across the same hillside lower down. Turn left and climb back up to the starting point.

Skyline Trail, Huckleberry Preserve

Oakland, San Francisco from Sequoia-Bayview Trail

Joaquin Miller & Dimond Canyon

Joaquin Miller Park was once part of a grove of giant redwoods that also covered Redwood Regional Park. These forests were all cut in the 1850's, leaving barren stump studded hillsides. The poet Joaquin Miller, after years of adventures in the wild west and success as a writer, in 1866 bought 80 acres in the Oakland Hills and settled there. "The Abbey" on Joaquin Miller Road was his home. He and his friends planted Monterey pines, cypress, olives and eucalyptus on his land. He had hoped to found an artist's commune here, but lack of cooperation forced him to give up this dream. The Oakland Park Department bought most of this land from Miller's widow in 1919, and it became the present park. The park contains many public facilities–picnic grounds, Woodminster Amphitheater, a horse show arena and several lodges. The park encompasses the canyon of Palo Seco Creek and the steep hillside up to Skyline Blvd. along the top of the hills. Much of this area is covered with beautiful second growth redwood forest, as well as the other trees that were planted here. The north slope of the canyon is mostly clear-cut and resprouting eucalpytus.

Below the Warren Freeway (state Highway 13), the creek joins a tributary to become Sausal Creek and continues down Dimond Canyon, a narrow strip of city park land, to Dimond Park. The Dimond

Canyon Trail makes it possible to walk on trail all the way from the busy Dimond district of Oakland through Joaquin Miller Park to Redwood Park and beyond. To get to the trail's beginning in Dimond Park, take I-580 south, and go left three blocks on Fruitvale Ave. AC Transit bus #53 goes by the park, and numbers 34, 57, 15, and N stop a block away on MacArthur Blvd. #18 goes up Leimert Blvd. from which the trail can be reached at its midpoint from Bridgeview Dr.

To get to Joaquin Miller Park, take Warren Freeway (13) to Joaquin Miller Rd. (or Fruitvale exit from I-580, cross Fruitvale and left on Champion, which becomes Lincoln Ave.). Turn left from Joaquin Miller Rd. onto Sandborn Drive through the central area of the park, or left on Skyline Blvd., which winds through the upper part. AC Transit buses #15A and V stop along Joaquin Miller Road, #18 goes up Castle Dr. stopping near the bottom of the Palos Colorados Trail and on Skyline Blvd. near the Skyline Trail.

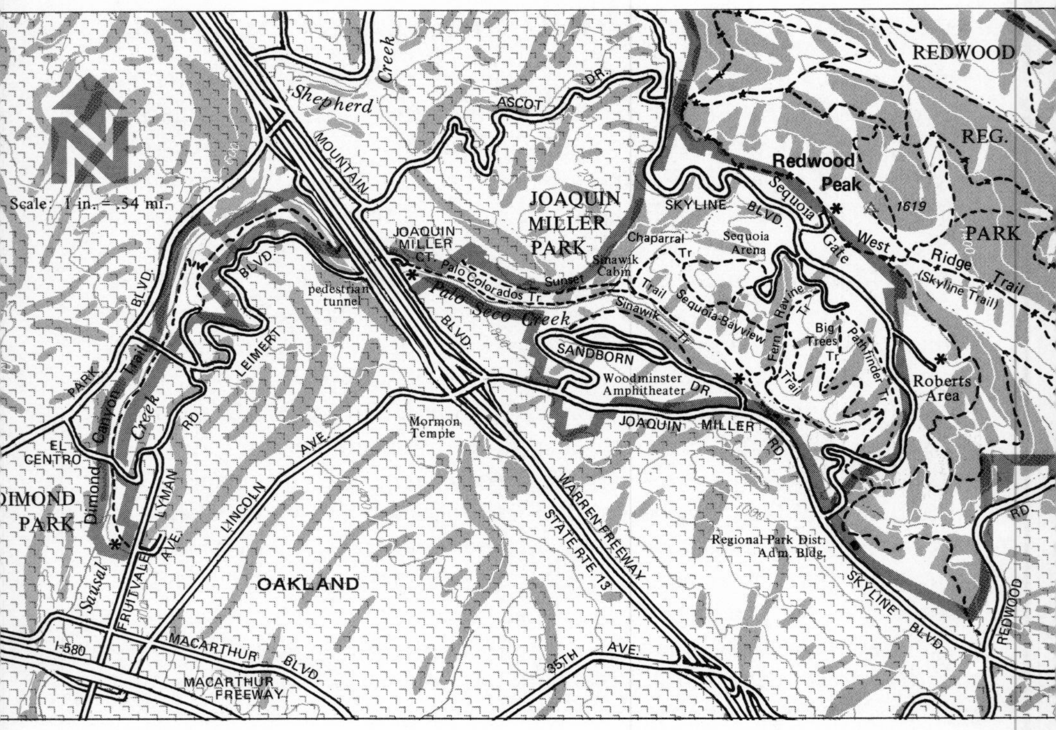

Dimond Canyon Trail *2.0 mi./400 ft. climb*

This trail goes up a shady little canyon to Joaquin Miller Park. It's not wilderness, but it has many nice spots and is easily accessible from Oakland.

From Dimond Park, follow the creek through the park and up the canyon, in places walking in the rocky creekbed (inadvisable after heavy rains). About ½ mile after going under the Leimert Blvd. bridge, switchback up the right bank and contour above the Montclair Golf Club driving range. Nearly to the freeway, descend again, cross the creek on a footbridge and come out on the frontage road, Monterey Blvd. Go to the right along the street, then under the freeway via a pedestrian tunnel. Cross Mountain Blvd., go down Joaquin Miller Court, to the beginning of the Palos Colorados Trail.

Palos Colorados & Sequoia-Bayview Trails *4.0 mi./800 ft. climb*

This route climbs up a wooded canyon, contours across a beautifully forested hillside, then drops back into the canyon. It tours most of Joaquin Miller Park.

From Joaquin Miller Road, take Mountain Blvd. half a mile to Joaquin Miller Court (or continue from the Dimond Canyon Trail, above). Start up the Palos Colorados Trail, crossing the creek and following it upstream. The banks are thickets of blackberries and horsetails, shaded by tall eucalyptus, bay and redwood. The narrow path forks, go left, climbing about 50 ft. above the creek, and traverse the very steep bank with arching bay trees, tall spindly redwoods, and mossy cliffs. A bridge crosses the creek to the wide Sinawik Trail. Continue along the left bank, not so steep now, turn right on a dirt road, then left on the Sunset Trail. Climb along the pine forested hillside. Two trails branch left; descend to lawns and picnic tables. Continue up the ravine as it steepens. Turn left on the Sequoia-Bayview Trail (to the right about ¼ mile it meets Skyline Blvd., making this trail easily accessible for short walks or jogging). Contour, winding in and out of several ravines. Through occasional openings in the woods, look down on Oakland. The forest is a mixture of redwood, pine and cypress. Cross the Fern Ravine Trail and pass through a grove of frost damaged eucalyptus. Turn left on the Chaparral Trail, follow this wide steep and dusty trail down through woods and brush. Turn right on a dirt road, then left by the Sinawik Cabin and pass it to reach the Palos Colorados Trail again. Return to the starting point.

Redwood

Redwood Regional Park was once a forest of giant redwoods, some of them probably taller than any tree now standing. Sailors in the early days used the redwoods as a landmark to guide them through the Golden Gate. Some of the stumps measured up to 21 ft. in diameter without the bark. A few of these trees were cut during the days of Spanish and Mexican control, but they hardly put a dent in the grove. Then cities and towns sprang up during the gold rush, and they needed lumber to build them. Steam sawmills were set up in the forest, and lumber was shipped out of the port of San Antonio (Oakland). At this time the population of the redwoods was greater than anywhere else in the East Bay. By 1860, not a redwood was left standing. Fortunately, redwoods grow new trees as shoots from the stumps, and today the second growth forest is cool, quiet and beautiful, though the trees are not large (about 3 ft. in diameter and 100 ft. tall). The forest covers the bottom and north facing slopes of the canyon of Redwood Creek (which includes most of the park), and the next canyon to the north, in which the small community of Canyon is located. For a very interesting history of the redwoods and Canyon, read *Canyon: The Story of the Last Rustic Community in Metropolitan America* by John Van Der Zee.

Redwood Park is one of the oldest regional parks, dating from the district's formation in 1934, and it is well developed. There are nice picnic areas, campgrounds for youth groups, a baseball diamond, an archery range, a swimming pool, and miles of trails for hikers and equestrians as well as beautifully unspoiled wild places.

The main entrance is on Redwood Road, reached from I-580 via 35th Ave. A short road leads from the entrance to a parking lot (parking fee). There is an entrance on the east ridge, reached by turning left from Redwood Road onto Pinehurst Road beyond the Main entrance, and winding to the top of the ridge. There are several entrances along Skyline Blvd. too. Going north from Redwood Road, you first come to the Regional Park District Administration Building, from which the Dunn Trail can be reached. Next, after Skyline turns left, is the Roberts Recreation Area (parking fee) where there is a swimming pool. A little further, just beyond the Rotary Day Camp, is the Sequoia Gate, where the archery range is located. A couple of miles further, there is the Skyline Gate—a wide turnout and parking lot with access to many trails. AC Transit provides special summer service to the Roberts Area

Redwood Creek, Stream Trail

from Fruitvale BART, 11 a.m.-6 p.m. daily. Also, bus #15A serves Skyline Blvd. near the EBRPD Administration Building.

Short Walks

The road up the canyon from the main entrance parking lot passes through the popular picnic areas and play areas and nice redwoods. The West Ridge Trail from the Skyline Gate is another good short walk, as well as the short climb up Redwood Peak from the Sequoia Gate.

Redwood Creek Headwaters *2.7 mi./700 ft. climb*

This route drops into the canyon and winds through the ravines of the uppermost branches of Redwood Creek. Here are the lushest redwoods of the park, dark forests undergrown with shaggy carpets of ferns and huckleberries, tiny streams splashing over mossy rocks.

Start from the Skyline Gate and take the left hand trail from the south end of the parking lot, the Stream Trail. Pass the "girl's camp" (a stone hut, restrooms, water), in a meadow. Go through cleared eucalyptus and into shady redwoods descending rather steeply to a small flat. Turn right, crossing the north fork of the creek and go up the south fork on the Tres Cendes Trail. After a short distance, turn left on the Redwood Peak Trail and go up a ravine. Turn right on the French Trail, climb a steep gully, go right at a fork, and cross a ravine thick with huckleberries. Come to a ridge, follow it a few feet and descend to the right into another ravine, down a tiny stream. Cross Redwood Creek's south fork and turn right on the Tres Cendes Trail. Go down the wide trail about 100 yards, and go left where the French Trail continues, a path traversing through broadleaf evergreens, then climbing along a pine forested ridge. Turn right on the West Ridge Trail and return to the Skyline Gate.

Through Redwood Park the Skyline Trail divides into two alternate routes. The West Ridge Trail is wide with gentle grades, the choice of those attempting to walk the whole trail or a long piece of it, those out for a casual stroll, joggers and equestrians. The alternative, the French Trail, is narrow and steep, and is the choice of those wishing to see the most beautiful forests of the park. A nice seven mile loop can be made by using both trails.

Skyline Trail—West Ridge Trail

4.6 mi./300 ft. climb southbound, 1000 ft. northbound

From the Skyline Gate follow the West Ridge Trail (right hand trail from the south end of the parking lot), contouring near the top of the Oakland hills through brush and Monterey pines. The second trail branching left is the alternate route (see below). Continue along the ridge and come to the Sequoia Gate. Follow a path along the top of the hill which soon becomes a wide trail. The Graham Trail branches right, leading to the Roberts Area. A path to the left joins the Redwood Peak Trail, and from it, Redwood Peak is an easy 100 foot climb to the left. Continue on the West Ridge Trail, coming out of the woods onto the gently rounded brushy ridge. Several trails branch right, the Sidney

Chown Trail branches left, then the Orchard Trail (by which the alternate route rejoins the West Ridge Trail). Descend the end of the ridge into Redwood Canyon, the same trail now named the Toyon Trail. Go right at the bottom on the Golden Spike Trail, parallel Redwood Road a ways, taking the left and lower trail, then cross the road to the MacDonald Gate of Anthony Chabot Regional Park. For the next section of the Skyline Trail, see p. 69.

Skyline Trail—French Trail

5.5 mi./500 ft. climb southbound, 1200 ft. northbound

As described above, follow the West Ridge Trail about a mile south of the Skyline Gate, then take the second left, the Tres Cendes Trail. Descend into the redwoods and turn right on the French Trail. Go up and down, in and out of ravines, traversing the side of the canyon and crossing several other trails, the Redwood Peak Trail, Mill Trail, Fern Trail, and Sidney Chown Trail. The dense redwoods begin to thin and oak, bay and madrone appear on the ridges. Turn right on the Orchard Trail and climb to meet the West Ridge Trail again. Go left, and continue as described for the first alternative, above.

East Ridge & Stream Trail *6.0 mi./800 ft. climb*

This route follows the long, brushy east ridge from the main entrance, with views of hills and canyons, then goes down Redwood Creek through peaceful redwood forest.

Start at the main entrance parking lot in the canyon. From the right side of the lot, follow the dirt road, the Canyon Trail, up a small wooded canyon. Turn left at the ridgetop, onto the East Ridge Trail. This fire road follows the ridge over gentle ups and downs, gradually climbing, in grass and brush with scattered oaks and redwoods. After a couple of miles, the Mill Trail branches left, descending to the Stream Trail. Continue into pine and eucalyptus to the Skyline Gate. Go left on the Stream Trail and descend into the canyon. Follow the creek through cool redwoods, still and quiet but for the call of a jay and the trickling creek. Cross the Mill Trail near the site of an old lumber mill where the big trees were cut up in the 1850's. Pass three stone huts that may be reserved for youth groups, and come to picnic areas, lawn and paved road. The road was open to cars to this point until 1972. Since then, this part of the park has been so much nicer. Pass more picnic areas, playground and ball field, and arrive back at the parking lot.

View down Grass Valley from MacDonald Trail

Anthony Chabot

Anthony Chabot Regional Park is a long sprawling area of stately eucalyptus forest and ravaged slopes of sprouting stumps, of rolling hills of coyote bush, oaks and vine thickets, of campgrounds, the jarring sounds of motorcycles and gunshots, and the winding blue waters of Lake Chabot.

This reservoir, named for its engineer, Anthony Chabot, was built in 1874, one of the first in California. The dam was made from earth washed from the hills by hydraulic nozzles like those used for gold mining and compacted by the hooves of wild horses driven back and forth over the dam. The reservoir is now used by EBMUD as a reserve supply of drinking water.

The park covers the southern extension of the Berkeley Hills, known here as the San Leandro Hills. It was originally called Grass Valley Regional Park, named after the long narrow valley which extends most of the length of the park, its creek emptying into an arm of Lake Chabot. Grass Valley used to be, as its name suggests, mostly grassland, but now much of it is covered with coyote bush. Large areas of hills, in Redwood and Tilden as well as in Chabot, have been rapidly taken over by brush, probably because cattle no longer graze here, and wildfires have been controlled.

This park does not compare with some of the others for scenic beauty. Its hills are not particularly high or rugged, much of them overgrown with brush or roughed up by eucalyptus logging, and a large area has been cut up with motorcycle trails. But first appearances can be deceptive. Away from the roads, there is lots of uncrowded country and abundant wildlife. And Lake Chabot is a real gem, a beautiful place to spend a lazy afternoon floating or fishing. Boats may be rented at the marina on Lake Chabot Road and there is a snack stand and tackle shop. Unfortunately, you may not swim in the lake. The park also contains the Willow Park Golf Course on Redwood Road with clubhouse, restaurant, swimming pool and driving range, the equestrian center on Skyline Blvd., which boards and rents horses, a marksmanship range, 67 acres of motorcycle trails, a family camping area and campgrounds for youth groups.

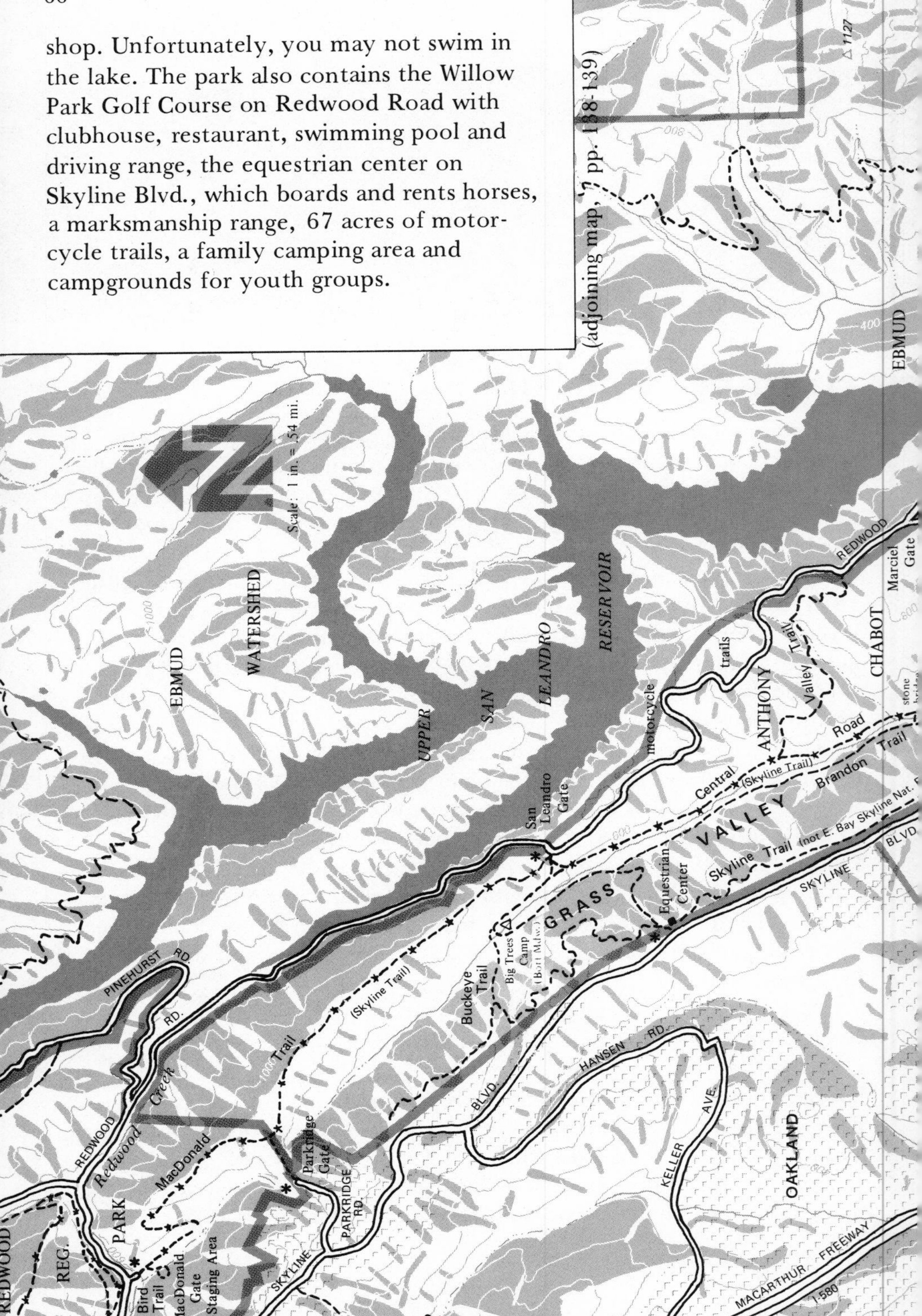

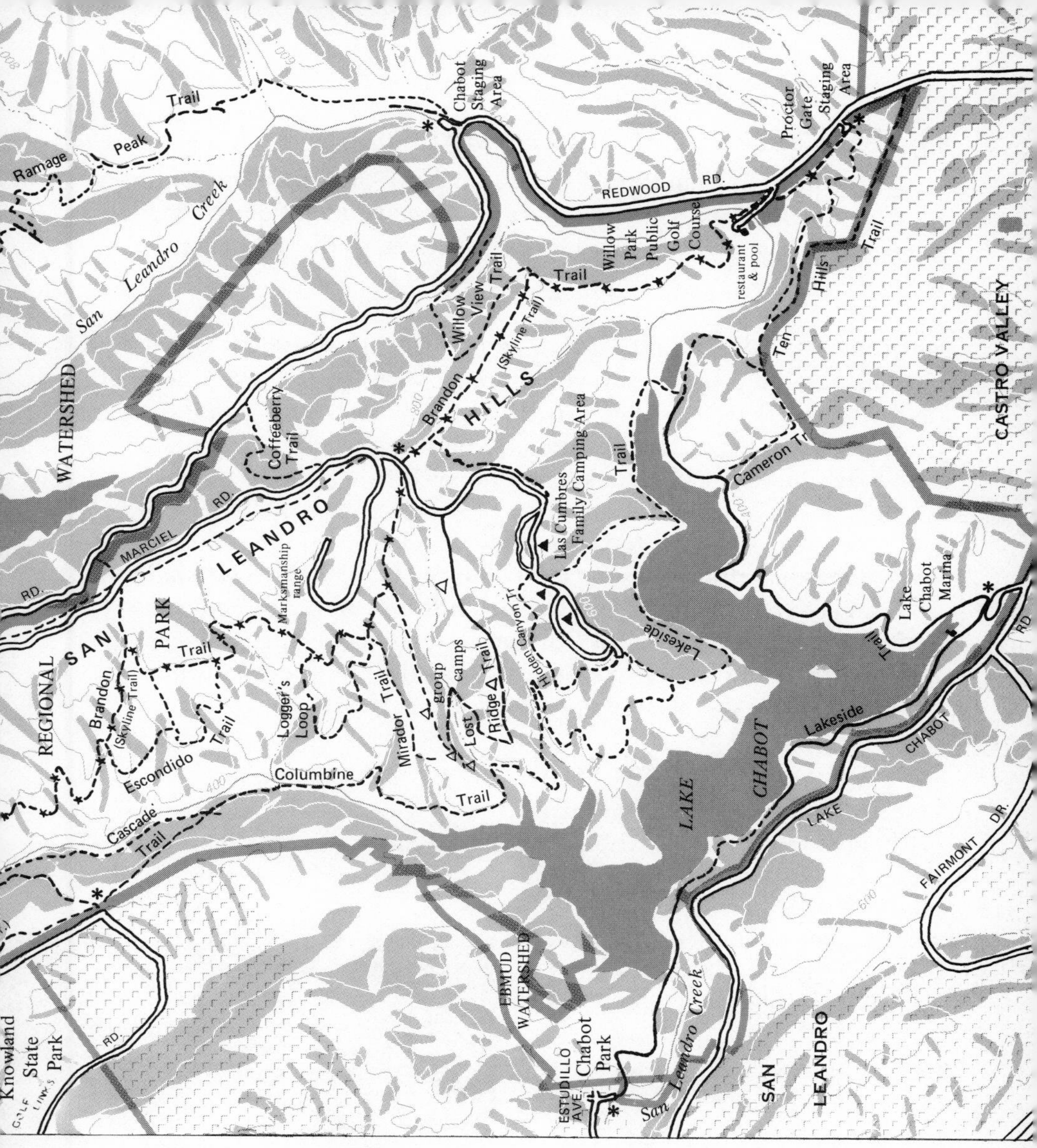

To get there, take 35th Ave. from I-580 to Redwood Road, which crosses Skyline Blvd. There are four entrances from Redwood Road, from north to south, MacDonald Gate, San Leandro Gate, Marciel Gate, and Proctor Gate. From Skyline Blvd., there is the Parkview Gate, the equestrian center and the Chabot Gate. To get to Lake Chabot, take I-580 to Estudillo Blvd. in San Leandro, and go east to Lake Chabot Road which leads to the marina. AC Transit busses 15A and 46A provide weekday access from Skyline Blvd., and there is special summer service to Lake Chabot from San Leandro BART, 11 a.m.- 6 p.m., daily.

Hidden Canyon Trail *1.1 mi./100 ft. climb*

Around the Las Cumbres Family Camping Area there is an interesting one mile long self-guiding nature trail, the Hidden Canyon Trail, a good way for campers to introduce themselves to the park's natural environment.

Lakeside Trail *5.5 mi./500 ft. climb eastbound, 400 ft. westbound*

This paved bicycle path is very popular with joggers and fishermen (and women) as well as bicyclists. It is an easy trail with gentle slopes from Chabot Park, a San Leandro city park at the end of Estudillo Ave., past the old earth fill dam and the well fished shores of Lake Chabot, to the Marina and on around the lake to its end. From here you may take either the Lakeside Trail which crosses the creek, goes back along the opposite shore and climbs to Las Cumbres Campground, or you may turn right and climb to the hilltop and continue on the Ten Hills Trail to the Proctor Gate on Redwood Road. At present, the western end of the trail is temporarily closed while the dam is being rebuilt. It is scheduled to re-open September 1981.

Cascade & Columbine Trails *7.9 mi./800 ft. climb*

This route down through lower Grass Valley and through the hills is recommended for those with plenty of adventurous spirit since parts of the trail exercise route finding ability as well as legs. Along the way is a pretty little waterfall, swampy willows, steep wooded hillsides overlooking Lake Chabot, and miles of eucalyptus forest.

From the Marciel Gate on Redwood Road, follow the Marciel Road until it splits; go left and park by the gate to Las Cumbres. Follow the Brandon Trail (East Bay Skyline Trail) west across the hill below the road to the marksmanship range. Wind through open eucalyptus forest with several trails branching left. After three miles, come to the bottom of the valley and turn left, leaving the Skyline Trail and crossing the

Falls, Cascade Trail

stone bridge. Just on the other side, turn left on a narrow path, the Cascade Trail. Follow the creek downstream past cascades and falls and traverse the hillside until a gate is encountered. Turn left on the Columbine Trail (to the right, the Cascade Trail climbs to the Chabot Gate), and descend to the creek, where the trail seems to disappear. Follow the creekbed about ¼ mile through willows, then climb a path up the left bank and traverse above the northern arm of Lake Chabot. The path is narrow and overgrown and is crossed by several paths leading from the group camps on the hill down to the water. Contour in and out of several ravines, one taking you a considerable distance inland, and then through eucalyptus forest, and come to Las Cumbres. Walk through the campground and then get on the trail which parallels the road on the right, climb around a grassy hill, and turn left on the Brandon Trail which shortly takes you back to the starting point.

Skyline Trail—MacDonald & Brandon Trails

8.7 mi./1200 ft. climb southbound, 1500 ft. northbound

This last section of the Skyline Trail leads from Redwood Park to Castro Valley, the entire length of Anthony Chabot Regional Park. It is a wide trail, good for horses, with relatively gentle grades after the first mile.

From the MacDonald Gate Staging Area off Redwood Road, follow the trail through vines and willows and up the canyon through brush and woods. A long switchback takes you near the top of a ridge, which you follow, still climbing. Level off and come to a saddle. A wide dirt road connects with Parkridge Road off Skyline Blvd. Grass Valley stretches into the distance to the south, and on the horizon, the ridges east of Hayward are blue lines floating on the haze. Follow the rounded ridge down into the valley. At the San Leandro Gate on Redwood Road, turn right, then left on the Central Road along the valley floor in grassland and brush. Eucalyptus forest begins abruptly like a curtain across the valley. On the right a stone bridge connects with the Brandon Trail and a road up to Chabot Gate. Stay left and begin climbing on the Brandon Trail. The trail goes gently up and down, winding in and out of ravines, several trails branching off. Pass the noisy marksmanship range and continue through grass and brush, crossing the Marciel Road. Soon there is a wide view to the south as you descend a ridge towards the green golf course in the valley with glimpses of Lake Chabot winding between the hills. Go through the golf course and continue parallel to Redwood Road to the Proctor Gate Staging Area, and the end of the 30 mile trail.

3. Central Contra Costa County

Briones

Briones Regional Park is sensuously rounded grassy hills exquisitely dabbed and sploched with oaks, a maze of ridges enclosing little hidden meadows and wooded canyons. Much of the park is undeveloped, uncrowded and beautifully natural, a delightful place to roam, especially in the winter and spring when everything is green.

Stretching across the park from east to west and curving south along the park's eastern boundary, are the Briones Hills. To the south they join Lafayette Ridge which overlooks the town of Lafayette. Bear Creek heads all along the hills and flows out of the southwest corner of the park into Briones Reservoir. To the east the streams drain into Walnut Creek and to the north, into Alhambra Creek.

To get to the most developed part of the park, the Bear Creek Entrance, take Freeway 24 through the tunnel to Orinda, turn left on Camino Pablo, right on Bear Creek Rd., and follow it past Briones Dam to the park entrance, a short road leading to parking lots and picnic areas.

The park may also be entered from the northern side from Martinez, the Alhambra Valley Entrance, by taking Freeway 4 to Martinez, turn-

ing south on Alhambra Ave. right on Alhambra Valley Rd., right at the intersection with Reliez Valley Rd. and left on Briones Rd., going up the hill and into the park to the road's end.

Another entrance on the eastern side in Pleasant Hill may be reached by taking Freeway 24 to Lafayette, turning left on Pleasant Hill Rd., left on Reliez Valley Rd., and several miles to a trail entrance on the left, opposite Gloria Terrace.

Short Walk—Nature Trail *.8 mi./200 ft. climb*

This is an easy walk through beautiful woods. Start at the parking lot at the end of the Bear Creek Entrance road. Follow the pavement to its end and take the path to the right, switchbacking down to a bridge across Bear Creek. The banks are green with ferns and vines and shaded by big oaks, bays and sycamores. Listen to the songs of many different birds. Traverse the far bank, heading downstream through shady woods. Cross the creek again and climb the bank to a picnic area near the start.

Mott Peak Loop *4.2 mi./800 ft. climb*

This moderately easy route tours some of the nicest parts of the park, gentle valleys, high ridges with distant views, and a couple of interesting ponds.

From the parking lot at the end of the Bear Creek Entrance, take the left-hand gravel road, the San Felipe Trail, which years ago was an unpaved county road connecting Briones Valley with Alhambra Valley. Cross open fields of weeds and thistles and wind through oaks along the steep creek bank. Climb along the hillside above the head of the valley and reach the top of the Briones Hills to be greeted with a view of Martinez and the Carquinez Straits. Turn left on the Briones Crest Trail and pass between a couple of ponds ringed with cattails, the Sindicich Lagoons. Climb to the ridge and turn left onto the Mott Peak Trail. A short distance south is Mott Peak, one of the high points of the park. Turn left again onto the Black Oak Trail, continue along the ridge, and descend to the left just short of Black Oak Knob, rejoining the San Felipe Trail and returning to the parking lot.

Briones Crest Trail *7.1 mi./1200 ft. climb*

This route covers a big hunk of beautiful, unspoiled country. It climbs a ridge from Bear Creek to the crest of the Briones Hills, then follows the rolling hilltops across the park and returns down a gentle valley.

View from San Felipe Trail

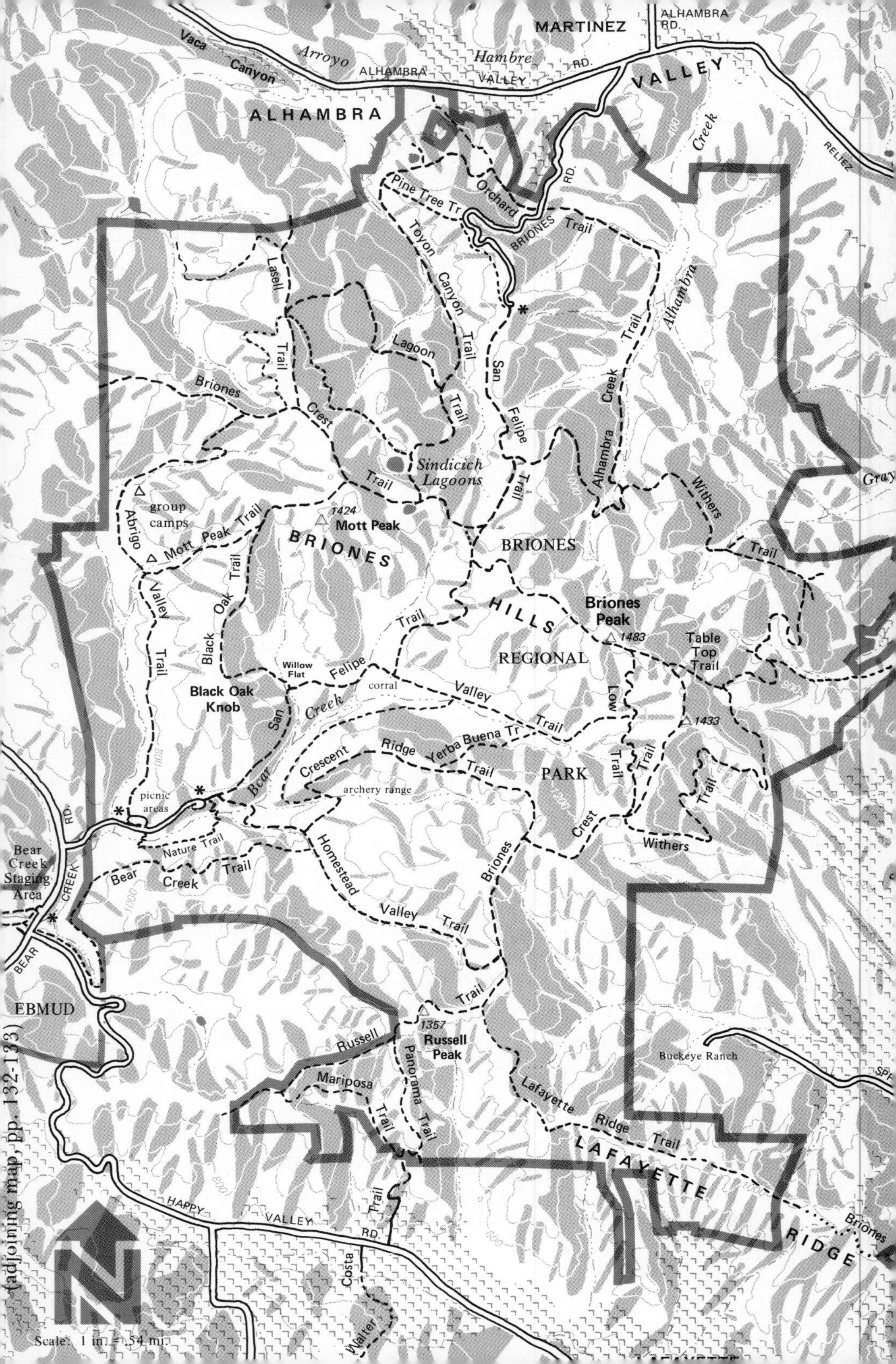

MARTINEZ
ALHAMBRA RD.
Vaca Canyon
Arroyo
Hambre
ALHAMBRA
VALLEY
RD.
VALLEY
ALHAMBRA
Creek
RELIEZ
Orchard
RD.
Pine Tree Tr
BRIONES Trail
Toyon Canyon Trail
Lasell Trail
Lagoon Trail
San Felipe Trail
Alhambra Creek Trail
Alhambra
Briones Crest Trail
Sindicich Lagoons
Withers Trail
Gray
group camps
Abrigo
Mott Peak Trail
1424
Mott Peak
BRIONES
BRIONES
HILLS
REGIONAL
PARK
Valley Trail
Black Oak Trail
Trail
Briones Peak
1483
Table Top Trail
Willow Flat
San Felipe
corral
Valley Trail
Black Oak Knob
Creek
Bear
1433
Low Trail
Trail
Crescent Ridge Trail
Yerba Buena Tr
archery range
Trail
picnic areas
Crest
Withers
Nature Trail
Homestead Valley Trail
Briones
RD.
Bear Creek Staging Area
CREEK
Bear Creek Trail
BEAR
EBMUD
Trail
1357
Russell Peak
Russell
Mariposa Trail
Panorama Trail
Buckeye Ranch
Lafayette Ridge Trail
LAFAYETTE RIDGE
Briones
HAPPY VALLEY RD.
Trail
Costa
Walter
(adjoining map, pp. 132-133)
Scale: 1 in. = .54 mi.

One of Sindicich Lagoons

View down Bear Cr. from Briones Pk.

Start at the first parking lot to the left of the Bear Creek Entrance road. Follow the road a short distance to the pavement's end, and take the right-hand gravel road, the Homestead Valley Trail, go along the creekbank beneath big bays and sycamores and climb into a flat meadow, Homestead Valley. Turn left, climb along the thistle covered hillside and along the crest of an oak studded ridge on the Crescent Ridge Trail. Reach the main crest, where a view opens to the east of Walnut Creek and Mt. Diablo. Turn left on the Briones Crest Trail and go up and down along the hilltops, slowly curving left around the head of the Bear Creek watershed. Keep to the ridge as trails branch off on either side. Pass a high point topped with an antenna, peak 1433, and ½ mile further, Briones Peak, the park's highest, just off the trail to the right. Descend gradually along the broad ridgetop. Turn right on the San Felipe Trail for a few yards, then left, continuing on the Briones Crest Trail. Pass the Sindicich Lagoons, go right at the next hilltop and slowly descend across rolling fields. After the Lassell Trail branches right, turn left on the Abrigo Valley Trail, leaving the crest, and drop into Abrigo Valley. Pass a little waterfall and down on the valley floor, a group camp (shelter, water, toilets). Continue down the valley, passing another camp where the Mott Peak Trail branches left. The valley narrows and the road follows the edge of the steep, heavily wooded bank of the creek. Come out at the parking lot, completing the loop.

North Side Loop *7.2 mi./1300 ft. climb*

This route starts at the Alhambra Valley Entrance, climbs nearly to the crest of the hills, then loops back down almost to the valley, crossing the entrance road, and climbing back up Alhambra Creek, tying together several of the park's newer trails. It goes from rolling grassland on the ridges to shady woods in the canyons and gentle hillsides of pine and eucalyptus near the valley.

From the end of Briones Road, follow the San Felipe Trail along the canyon side and ridge nearly to the crest. Turn right on the Briones Crest Trail, then right again beside the smaller of the two Sindicich Lagoons. At the larger pond, turn left on a path which contours across a pleasant landscape of woods and grassy swales. Turn right on the Lagoon Trail and descend steeply, then climb slightly, turn left on the Toyon Canyon Trail, and drop into the canyon. Almost to the bottom, come out of the canyon above a ranch. The Pine Tree Trail branches right leading back up to the road's end. Now on the Orchard Trail, pass a small pond and go through a ranchyard to cross Briones Road. Descend gently into the valley of Alhambra Creek, and turn right, up the valley on the Alhambra Creek Trail. Climb through dense woods out of the canyon, turn right on the San Felipe Trail and return to the starting point.

Withers Trail Loop *8.3 mi./1800 ft. climb*

The Withers Trail winds along the east slope of the Briones Hills, a patchwork of chaparral and beautiful woods of oak and bay, quite different terrain from the grassy hills west of the crest. This route combines the woods of the Withers Trail with the ridgetops of the Briones Crest trail for a varied and interesting trip.

From Reliez Valley Road at Gloria Terrace, go west through a gate and up a path, the East Trail, along a low ridge overlooking a new development. Join a dirt road and continue steeply up the canyon to a fork. Turn left on the Withers Trail, climb through woods, and turn left near a broken windmill (to the right is the Table Top Trail leading up to the crest). Contour across a couple of ravines and around a spur into a bowl at the foot of the precipitous chaparral clad face of peak 1433. Climb a ridge and turn right on the Briones Crest Trail. Follow the crest north past peak 1433 and Briones Peak, down to the San Felipe Trail, and turn right. Make another right onto the Alhambra Creek Trail, and descend into the heavily wooded canyon. At the bottom, turn right on the Withers Trail and climb over a ridge and down across the oak wooded hillside and into a ravine. Turn right and contour to a spur where a couple of trails branch left, and climb around another spur and down into the canyon. Turn left on the East Trail, and return to the start.

Lafayette Ridge Trail

4.3 mi./700 ft. climb eastbound, 1000 ft. westbound–to Pleasant Hill Rd.; 3.5 mi. from Bear Cr. Tr. at Homestead Valley

This route is the first section of the regional trail connection between Briones and Mt. Diablo State Park, a trail which should be complete in the near future. At present, the trail goes along the top of Lafayette Ridge, grassy hilltops looking right down on the town of Lafayette, and only one small gap, soon to be filled, remains in the extension of the trail to the end of the ridge at Pleasant Hill Road.

If you are starting from Briones, from the parking lot at the Bear Creek Entrance, take the right-hand gravel road, the Homestead Valley Trail, to Homestead Valley. If you are continuing from EBMUD trails around Briones Reservoir, you will reach Homestead Valley on the Bear Creek Trail (see p.134). Go up the valley on the Homestead Valley Trail and climb steeply to the crest. Turn right on the Russell Peak Trail, and go about ¼ mile to the hilltop where Lafayette Ridge joins the Briones Crest and descend a steep path to the left onto the ridge (the Russell Peak Trail goes on to Russell Peak and a trail loop down the southern slope of the ridge). Follow a narrow path which contours around the hilltops overlooking Lafayette a mile and a half to the park boundary. Until this section of trail is complete to Pleasant Hill Road, retrace your steps to Briones.

Briones to Mt. Diablo Tr.—through Walnut Creek

4.6 mi./200 ft. climb eastbound, 500 ft. westbound

This is the first officially open section of the 13 mile trail between Briones and Mount Diablo. From a new staging area on Pleasant Hill Road in Lafayette, across from Acalanes High School, the trail winds over Acalanes Ridge into Walnut Creek and down the EBMUD Mokelumne Aqueduct right-of-way, then as a level paved trail along the Contra Costa Canal across town to Heather Farms Park near Ygnacio Valley Rd. The trail is separated from traffic all the way, including a 150 ft. tunnel under North Main St.

Walter Costa Trail

The City of Lafayette has recently opened a trail connecting Lafayette Reservoir to Briones Regional Park, the Walter Costa Trail. The trail is intended more as a pedestrian access to the parks than as a hiking trail, and much of it is along roads and driveways.

San Pablo Reservoir

This long reservoir, owned by EBMUD, is now temporarily closed to fishing and boating, but is scheduled to re-open April 1981. When it does, boats can be rented at the recreation area on San Pablo Dam Road and you may fish from the shores or boat. There is a road along the west bank, the Old San Pablo Trail, which is good for cycling, riding or walking, but is not very peaceful because it is so near the sounds of speeding traffic on San Pablo Dam Road. With a permit from EBMUD, several trails may be followed from the reservoir. The Eagles' Nest Trail leaves the Old San Pablo Trail about ½ mile northwest of the recreation area and climbs the hill to join Nimitz Way in Wildcat Canyon Regional Park. The Inspiration Trail and the Oursan Trail leave the Old San Pablo Trail near the southeast end of the reservoir and both are described on pp. 132-134.

Lafayette Reservoir

This is a pleasant little lake in a setting of gentle oak studded hills. It is owned by EBMUD for storage of water from the Sierra, and it is open to the public as a recreation area. There is good fishing, and you may rent a boat (or bring your own), but no motor boats are allowed, so it is nice and quiet. Many take advantage of the paved trail around the reservoir for walking, jogging or cycling.

To get there, take Freeway 24 towards Walnut Creek, exit on Mt. Diablo Blvd., and go about a mile to the entrance on the right. Or walk 1¼ miles from the Lafayette BART Station.

Shore Trail *2.7 mi./100 ft. climb*

This is a paved road circling the lake. It is great for bicycles and is an easy, scenic walk too. From the parking lot on the dam, just follow the road along the shore, which is lined with cattails and willows. All the

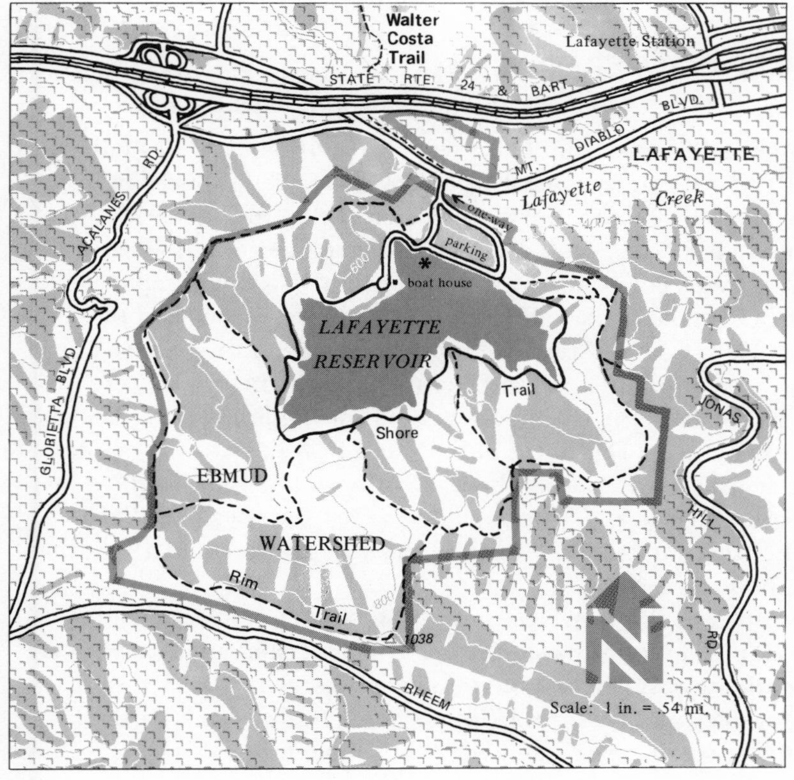

way around, there are changing vistas of colorful sailboats on sparkling blue water and lightly wooded hills. Several trails branch off which connect with the rim trail. Try this walk on a wet winter day sometime when most other trails are too muddy.

Rim Trail *4.8 mi./1000 ft. climb*

This is a dirt road which follows the ridges encircling the reservoir. It has lots of ups and downs, but no long climbs, and it provides many views of the reservoir as well as the surrounding suburbs.

From the parking lot, go toward the boathouse a few yards, then turn right. Soon find yourself overlooking the reservoir. The hills are grassy with patches of coyote bush and live oaks. Go south over rolling hills near suburban backyards. Climb along a steep-sided ridge overlooking a brush filled valley at the head of the reservoir, to a high hill. Take in the panoramic view, drop steeply, and pass many new tract homes, look down on Lafayette, and gradually descend back to the dam.

Lafayette-Moraga Trail

5.5 mi./300 ft. climb southbound, downhill northbound

A familiar sight in my childhood were little electric engines pulling a few boxcars or sometimes a passenger car through the suburbs of Lafayette. The Sacramento Northern Railroad was built in 1913 and at first operated all the way from Oakland to Sacramento, but from 1940 went only to Port Chicago and dropped its passenger service. Its route from Oakland started from the Montclair district and tunneled under the hills to Canyon, then went on to Moraga, a tiny village at the time, Lafayette, Walnut Creek and Concord. After the tracks were pulled up in the 50's, the roadbed was used for the lines of the Central Contra Costa Sanitary District, EBMUD, and PG&E. With the cooperation of these utilities in sharing the right-of-way, and joint funding by the cities of Lafayette and Moraga and the East Bay Regional Park District, the trail was built and opened through Lafayette in 1976, then extended to Moraga in 1978.

The resulting trail is now very popular with area residents, and it should be. Its 5½ miles of paved bicycle trail and accompanying horse and foot path are easily accessible to many, very gently graded (a real plus for bicycles), and pass through nice countryside—back yards and horse pastures, grazing cattle and vistas of rolling hills.

To get to the north end of the trail, take Freeway 24 to Pleasant Hill Rd., go south and turn left on Olympic Blvd. The trail begins at the intersection with Reliez Station Rd. To get to the south end of the trail, take Freeway 24 to Orinda, go right on Moraga Way to Moraga. Turn left on Moraga Rd. and find the end of the trail at the intersection with St. Mary's Rd. The trail may also be entered from numerous cross streets along the way.

Future park district plans include the extension of this trail north and south to connect Briones Regional Park with Las Trampas Regional Wilderness. The following trail, with a little road walking and an EBMUD trails permit, already makes this southern connection to Las Trampas possible, though not very direct.

Old Moraga Ranch Trail

1.7 mi./800 ft. climb to St. Mary's Peak; 4.1 mi. to Rocky Ridge Tr.

From Bollinger Canyon Road behind St. Mary's College, this trail climbs up into beautiful hills, coming out on top of St. Mary's Peak right above the college, then heads south to connect with EBMUD's Rocky Ridge Trail, which leads over many rough miles to Las Trampas Regional Wilderness. The walk up to the peak and back makes for a very enjoyable few hours.

From the Lafayette-Moraga Trail and St. Mary's Road ¼ mile north of the college, where the road dips, walk or drive up Bollinger Canyon Road to the end of the pavement, continue walking up the private road ¼ mile and turn right on the trail. Climb up a wooded ravine which opens up into brush and grassland. Ascend steeply to the ridge and go down the other side into a lovely valley. Pass to the right of a ramshackle barn and go up the ravine behind it. Another stiff climb takes you to the top of St. Mary's Peak for a panoramic view starring the Spanish style buildings of the college.

Oak, Devil's Hole

Las Trampas

Las Trampas Regional Wilderness is the heart of a wild, rugged region of cattle ranches and watershed. It is crossed by Las Trampas Ridge and higher Rocky Ridge, just over 2000 ft. Between them is Bollinger Canyon where most of the trails begin.

There are billowy grass covered hillsides, steep chaparral clad slopes, rugged sandstone cliffs, lots of wildlife, and a network of well marked trails. The immense forces shaping the earth are readily apparent in this area. The strata of the two ridges were folded past the breaking point, and Rocky Ridge was forced up over part of Las Trampas Ridge. The fault along which this occurred is called the Bollinger Thrust. These hills hold a special meaning for me, as I hiked around here often as a kid, but I think any aware person will share the special beauty of these gentle woods, sunny fields and bold ridges.

To get there, go to Crow Canyon Road by either taking I-580 south to Castro Valley or taking Freeway 24 east, I-680 south to San Ramon. About a mile west of San Ramon on Crow Canyon Rd., Bollinger Canyon Road turns north. Follow it to its end at the park entrance and parking lot.

The park may also be entered by trail from Danville. From downtown, go north on Danville Blvd., left on Del Amigo Rd., right on Starview to its end, where the Del Amigo Trail starts.

South, along the ridge, from Las Trampas Peak

The Little Hills Ranch Regional Recreation Area a half mile down the road from Las Trampas is a group picnic area available by reservation only (582-1630).

Short Walks

From the parking lot, follow the Creek Trail through shady bay trees along the creek for half a mile, cross the creek and return on the Valley Trail, an easy walk with plenty to see.

Another walk that is not quite so short or easy, but is beautifully rewarding, is the Mahogany Trail, a steep mile and a half. From the parking lot, go back down the road a short distance and follow the Chamise Trail up the hillside to the left. Turn right on the Mahogany Trail, switchback down the steep bank of a ravine with many wildflowers, and climb along a tiny creek. Pass a small falls and enter a pretty little chaparral covered valley. Climb a little more, turn left on the Chamise Trail, and descend back to the road.

Las Trampas Peak *3.8 mi./1000 ft. climb*

This route gives one a close look at the varied terrain of the Wilderness, from gentle valley to rugged ridge, grassland and chaparral to thick woods. It follows Bollinger Creek to its headwaters, climbs Las Trampas

Ridge to its highest point, Las Trampas Peak, with an impressive view, then it follows the sharp ridge back.

From the parking lot, follow the Valley Trail along the creek up the gentle valley to its head. Turn right on the Grassland Trail and climb into chaparral across the steep flank of the ridge. At the top, turn left on the Ridge Trail above a rugged canyon leading down to Alamo. Climb another 100 feet to Las Trampas Peak (which is outside of the park, but it is not fenced or posted—the landowner has apparently chosen to ignore the use of this short stretch of trail by hikers). Rest and enjoy the extensive view. Go back along the ridge, staying left past the trail you came up on, and going left on the Hiker's Trail. Traverse along the east side of the ridge in broadleaf evergreen woods, the trail narrow and rough in places. The Costanoan Trail branches right leading across a saddle to nearby Eagle Peak. Come back onto the ridge, open and grassy in places, and turn right on the Chamise Trail. Descend through chaparral into Bollinger Canyon. Go right on Bollinger Canyon Road a short distance back to the parking lot.

Sulfur Springs & Danville Overlook *3.8 mi./1200 ft. climb*

This somewhat strenuous route leads up and down beautiful ridges and ravines on both sides of Las Trampas Ridge. Start at the parking lot and follow Bollinger Canyon Road back a couple hundred yards, go left up the hill on the Chamise Trail and climb through chaparral. At the top of the ridge, turn right on the Gooseberry Trail. Pass above several high, vertical slabs of sandstone, and follow the narrow ridgecrest, then the woods just below it. Descend a steep hillside to a four-way junction. Go left on the Sulfur Springs Trail, descending through oak woodland to a canyon where Sulfur Spring trickles out of a pipe into old bathtubs. Follow a dirt road up the beautiful little canyon, then climb the grassy spur to the east. The town of Danville is directly below. To the left, the Del Amigo Trail leads down to the Starview Drive Entrance. Turn right on the Summit Trail, a dirt road climbing the spur to the main ridge. When the crest is reached, turn right on the Vista Trail, another dirt road. Follow the ridge west to Oak Circle (a vague circle of oaks on a grassy hill), where you leave the road, following a path to the left a hundred feet or so back to the four-way junction. Turn left on the Trapline Trail, descend the west slope of the ridge on a rough path through chaparral. Climb the spine of a sandstone outcrop and descend again through oaks and bays into a steep ravine. Turn left on the Mahogany Trail, left on the Chamise Trail, and return to the parking lot.

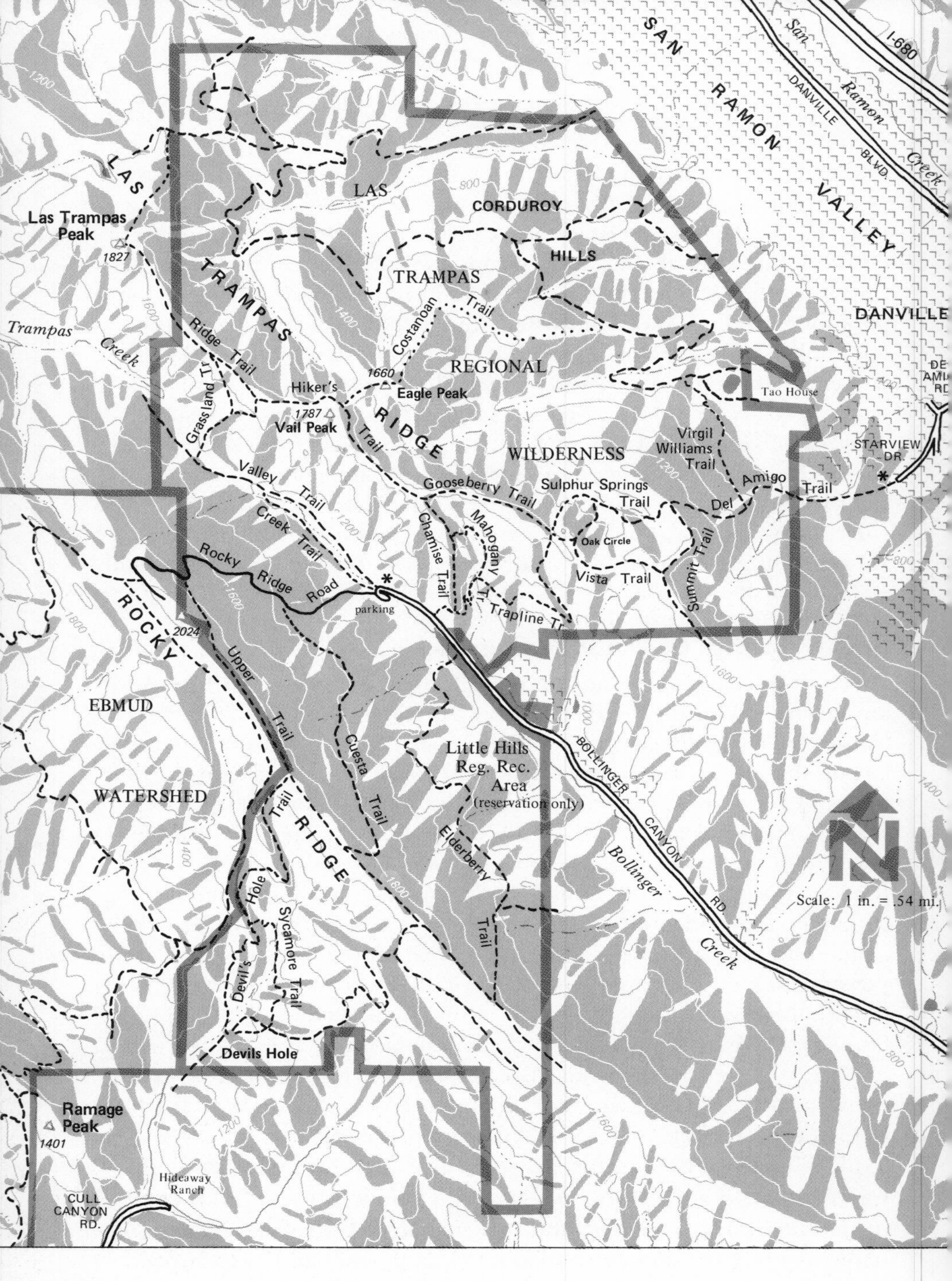

Upper Trail, Rocky Ridge, looking north. Mt. St. Helena on horizon

Devil's Hole *5.8 mi./2000 ft. climb*

This route includes two strenuous thousand foot climbs—first up the east slope of Rocky Ridge, then down the west slope, and back over the ridge again. It is well worth the effort, however. The view from the top is spectacular and the jagged sandstone outcrops and steep wooded ravines on the west side of the ridge are equally impressive.

Start from the parking lot and follow the paved road, the Rocky Ridge Road. It climbs rather steeply up the side of the ridge. Near the top, turn left on a path, the Upper Trail, and traverse below the antennae on the very summit (years ago the site of a missile base radar). Soon reach the crest of the ridge, with its extensive view. All around are waves of hills and the bay stretches across a wide piece of the western horizon. Mt. Diablo rises high above the chaparral of Las Trampas Ridge to the east. Take a close look at the sandstone exposed here—it is crowded with fossil sea shells. Follow the crest, then turn right on the Devil's Hole Trail and follow it down the far side of the ridge, just below sandstone outcrops pitted with wind caves and turkey vultures circling nearby. Cross this rocky spur into chaparral. The Sycamore Trail branches left. Pass around another spur and drop to a green and ferny glen with a small creek in a rocky bed, Devil's Hole. Go down the creek a short distance and turn left on the Sycamore Trail. The Devil's Trail continues down to Hideaway Ranch at the end of Cull Canyon Road where horses may be rented. Climb the opposite bank then contour left along the hillside through chaparral and oak woodland. Cross a

trickle of a creek, follow it downstream a short distance, cross another trickle that falls down a 30 ft. smooth sandstone wall. Soon cross the larger creek again and climb back up the Devil's Hole Trail. Retrace your steps back over the ridge from here.

If you have a trail permit from EBMUD, the trails of the watershed area west of Rocky Ridge are also accessible (see pp. 135-141). Beyond the gate near the top, Rocky Ridge Road continues as the Rocky Ridge Trail. It climbs to the summit, then continues as a dirt road down the west face of the ridge and eventually reaches Moraga. The Rocky Ridge Loop Trail parallels the Upper Trail along the ridgetop, goes down the west slope beside the Devil's Hole Trail and loops across the west face of the ridge to meet the Rocky Ridge Trail. The Ramage Peak Trail heads southwest and eventually reaches Castro Valley.

Corduroy Hills *9.4 mi./2300 ft. climb*

A long winding dirt road through the beautifully wooded "Corduroy Hills" area at the northern end of the park may be reached from Danville via the Virgil Williams Trail. There is no provision for parking at the trailhead at the end of Starview Drive. Limited roadside parking space exists, however.

From the trailhead, start up the Del Amigo Trail, crossing a small creek and climbing steeply. About halfway up the ridge, turn right on the Virgil Williams Trail, a narrow path easily missed in the tall grass. Traverse the hillside through oak woodland and descend to a dirt road (just below is the Tao House, the former home of playwright Eugene O'Neil, which is a national historical site). Turn left, cross the canyon and climb the other side, up a ridge, then traverse, going in and out of several ravines. Cross a meadow, 20 years or so ago the site of an unsuccessful oil well, and head into a canyon. A road branches right. Wind around the head of the canyon and climb to a ridge leading up to Las Trampas Peak.

As mentioned above, the peak is just outside the park boundary but not fenced or posted. From the peak, go south along the ridge (the Ridge Trail, Hiker's Trail, Gooseberry Trail, Vista Trail, and Summit Trail) and down the Del Amigo Trail, completing a long loop.

Another way to reach the Corduroy Hills area is the Costanoan Trail which is more of a cross country route than a trail. From the Hiker's Trail the Costanoan Trail climbs Eagle Peak, and a path descends the very steep east slope a ways. Follow the ridges east to connect with the dirt road into Corduroy Hills.

4. Southern Alameda County Hills

Cull Canyon

Cull Canyon Regional Recreation Area is a small reservoir and swimming lagoon in the hills of Castro Valley. The reservoir was built by the Alameda County Flood Control and Water Conservation District and developed by the East Bay Regional Park District for recreational use. The park opened in 1964 and is operated under an inter-agency agreement between the two districts. It's a nice place to fish or swim.

Cull Canyon has recently lost much of its appeal because of park district sell-outs. The aborted construction of a water slide (which has relocated to Shadow Cliffs in Pleasanton) has left a large excavation, and worse yet, the district allowed the destruction of a beautiful little valley which was nice for picnicking or short hikes, so that a road could be built through the park to a new residential development.

To get there, take Crow Canyon Rd. from I-580, turn left on Cull Canyon Rd. which leads to the park entrance.

Don Castro

Don Castro Regional Recreation Area is, like Cull Canyon, a small reservoir and swimming lagoon built and operated by EBRPD and the county Flood Control District, also a park since 1964. It is located in the eastern part of Hayward, right next to I-580. Besides the popular swimming pond, there are nice picnic areas and a pleasant 1.6 mile trail around the shore.

To get there, take the Crow Canyon Exit from I-580 and turn right on Center St., left on Kelly St., left on Woodroe Ave. AC Transit bus #95 takes you to Kelly and Woodroe, ½ mile from the park.

Hayward Greenbelt Trail *6.3 mi./1000 ft. climb*

This trail throuth the wooded canyon of Ward Creek in the Hayward Hills, though by no means wilderness, goes through some beautiful places and is nice for walking, jogging or riding. Take I-580 to Hayward, Foothill Blvd. through the downtown area, left on Mission Blvd., then left into the parking lot of the Hayward Plunge and Memorial Park. Or, from the Hayward BART Station, take the AC Transit bus #82 southbound on Mission Blvd.

Walk straight back through Memorial Park to find the trail, identified as the Wally Wickander Trail, leading up along the creek. Climb gradually up the shady canyon, cross a dry dam, traverse a brushy hillside, and pass behind several backyards to Campus Drive. Cross the street, go a few yards to the right, and continue on the trail up the canyon through beautiful woods. After a considerable distance, come out into brush and grassland and climb to Oaks Drive. Cross the street and follow Durham Way a hundred yards or so, then turn left on the trail down into the wooded canyon of another branch of Ward Creek. Pass trails branching right leading a short ways up into East Avenue Park, and continue down the shady canyon to Campus Drive, completing the loop, and return to the Plunge.

Sycamore leaf, Ward Creek

Near Gossip Rock, Dry Creek Pioneer

Garin & Dry Creek Pioneer

East of Hayward and Union City are two adjoining parks in the beautiful canyons and hills of Walpert Ridge, the first range rising from the plain, overlooking the southern half of the bay.

Garin Regional Park, which has been open for hiking for a few years, has been recently developed with a new entrance, picnic areas, play field, a fishing pond, an old barn and an exhibit of historic farming implements. The surrounding area of gently contoured hills of waving grass, wooded ravines, birds and flowers, has a feeling of seclusion unexpected so near the city.

Just southeast of Garin, Dry Creek Pioneer Regional Park was the very generous gift of Mildred and Jeannette Meyers, sisters whose grandparents sailed around the Horn more than 100 years ago to settle in these hills. From the early days, the family weclomed others to share in the enjoyment of the land, and they have continued that tradition by making the largest donation of land to the park district since its foundation in 1934. This park, together with Garin, offers a lot of fine country to explore.

While in this area, be sure to appreciate the abundant wildlife, clear flowing streams and unspoiled views to the east. In a few years they

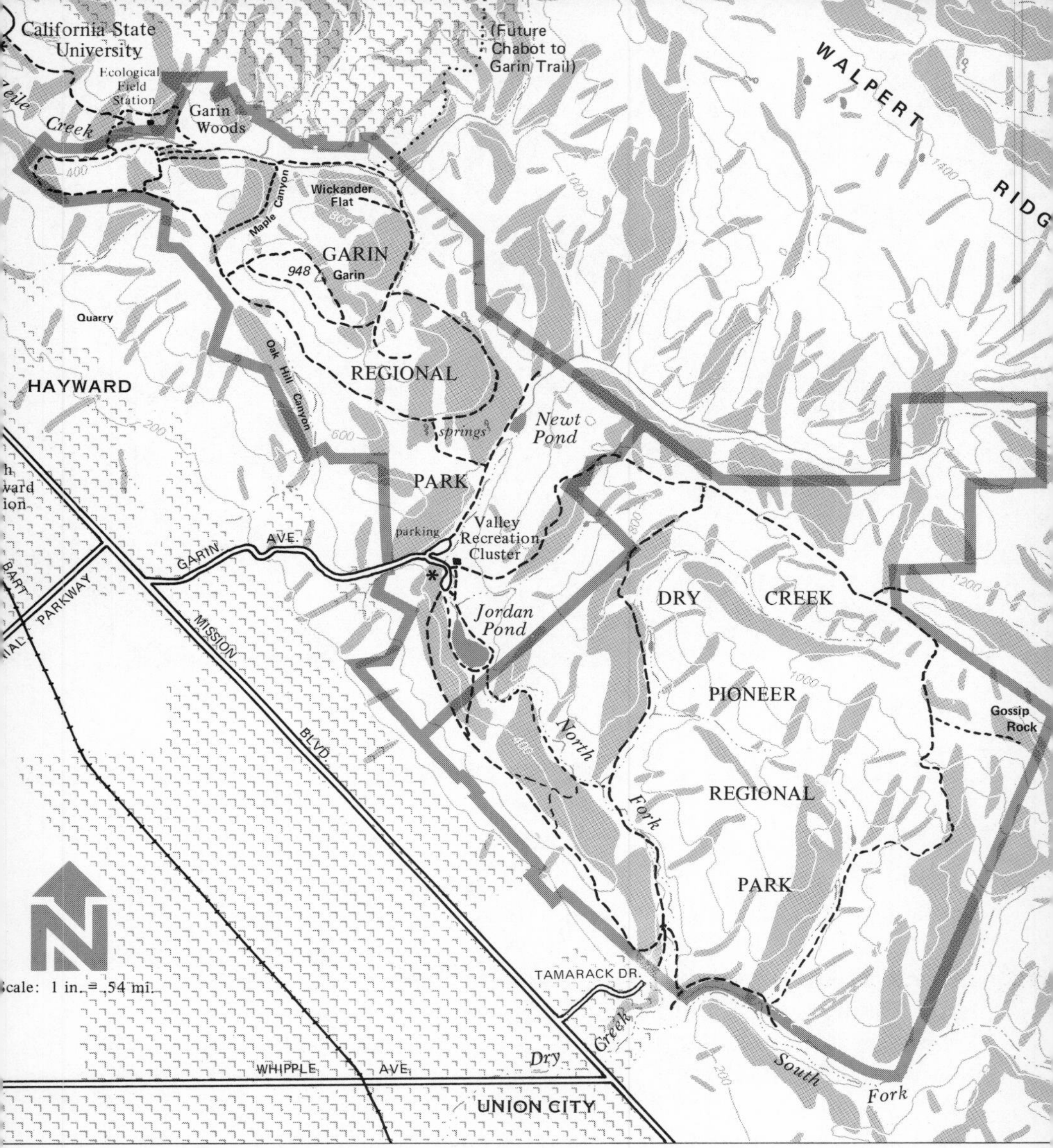

may not be there. The city of Hayward has made an unfortunate decision, despite much protest from its citizens, to allow development of all of the gently rolling crest of Walpert Ridge, development which will spoil the eastern viewshed of most of the park, which will cut off wildlife access from the larger wild area to the east, and which will most likely cause siltation of the streams of the park and kill aquatic life as has happened with development above Zeile Creek in the north end of Garin.

To get there, take I-580 to Hayward, follow Foothill Blvd., go left on Mission Blvd., and after a couple of miles, turn left on Garin Ave. which takes you to the park entrance for both parks. The Northern end of Garin Park may also be reached through California State University land (see Garin Woods, below). The old entrance to Garin from Calhoun Street is being closed because of difficulties in patrolling an extra park entrance. From the South Hayward BART Station, you may take the AC Transit bus #82 south on Mission Blvd. to Garin Ave., and walk about a mile to the park entrance.

Short Walks

A stroll around Jordan Pond, nicely landscaped for picnicking and fishing, is pleasant and easy. A walk up the valley on the left as you enter the park takes you past little Newt Pond to a beautiful stretch of Dry Creek near the park boundary.

Creek & Ridge *3.4 mi./700 ft. climb*

This moderately easy route will show you some of the best of both parks, from beautiful little Dry Creek to a high ridge with spacious views. From the parking lot, cross the creek and head to the right beside the play field to Jordan Pond. Pass the dam and continue down along the creek, crossing it several times (wet feet after lots of rain) as it meanders through beautiful open riparian woods with large oaks and sycamores. Where the trail climbs a hillside set with logs as steps, go left instead, cross the creek once more and come to a dirt road not far from a barn. Turn left, climbing beside a lovely little canyon to the top of a high ridge overlooking Hayward and Union City. Turn left and descend along the ridge, winding back down to the recreation area.

Garin Hill *3.2 mi./600 ft. climb*

This loop through the center of Garin Park features good views of all the South Bay. From the left (north) side of the parking lot, follow the road up the valley and turn left up the hill just short of Newt Pond. Go right and contour above the pond and into a peaceful oak wooded ravine. Climb to a small grassy swale and go right. Turn right again and soon the whole panorama of cities and hills unfolds as you reach the top of the hill. Descend the other side, passing a road branching left, and turn left a few yards further. Go over a gentle hill and down across the hillside to complete the loop and return to the parking lot.

Gossip Rock *6.0 mi./1300 ft. climb*

This route takes you along grassy ridges and green valleys around beautifully unspoiled Dry Creek Pioneer Park, giving panoramic views and a look at the Gossip Rock, long ago an Indian gathering place where acorns were ground in bedrock mortars and gossip exchanged.

From the parking lot, pass the barn and go straight across the field and up around the hill directly east. Climb to the ridge and continue southeast along its gently rolling crest with higher Walpert Ridge on the left and Union City spread below to the right. Descend slightly across a gentle saddle to a knoll and bear left, going cross country down its brow to the Gossip Rock. Return to the knoll and continue on the dirt road which drops across its southeast side, down a spur, and into a wooded little canyon. At the bottom, turn right on a gravel road, then right on another gravel road. Cross another road (which leads up the creek) near the end of Tamarack Drive, climb the hillside just above houses and follow a low grassy ridge northwest a couple of miles back to the parking lot.

Garin Woods *2.9 mi./500 ft. climb*

This pleasant and fairly easy loop begins at the Cal State Hayward parking lot, and goes through university land into the northern corner of Garin Park.

To get to the starting point, from Mission Blvd., go up Harder Rd. to the campus and into the parking lot to the right. Or, from the Hayward BART Station take the AC Transit bus #91A to the university.

From the end of the parking lot follow a gravel road through a gate and down around the hillside to a point just short of the Ecological Field Station where a sign indicates trails leaving the road. Go left across the hill above the station, across a little creek and a little further to Zeile Creek. Go upstream a short ways to the base of the massive fill of a new development, cross the creek and climb up a wild little ravine shaded by broadleaf evergreens. Out of the woods, go right on a dirt road, come to a cluttered ranchyard, and turn right, descending to the end of the road, go left on a path, then right, re-crossing Zeile Creek and completing the loop.

Mission Peak

Mission Peak

Mission Peak, one of the most prominent landmarks east of the bay, sticks its pointed head above a massive block of earth thrust steeply out of the plain. The view from the 2517 ft. peak is spectacular. You look almost straight down on the tiny streets and houses of Fremont, across the winding sloughs and marshes of the south end of the bay, to most of the Bay Area spread out around the horizon. It is well worth the more than two thousand foot climb to see.

Other trails in Mission Peak Regional Preserve go into the lower hills north of Ohlone College and you may explore the high rolling ridge and precipitous slopes more recently acquired south of the peak. Most of the preserve is grassland, with oaks and bays in the ravines and many sedimentary outcroppings. The southwest face of the peak is so steep that much of it is exposed rock.

The updrafts formed as air moves over the peak are very popular with glider pilots and their graceful aircraft are quite a sight as they quietly soar nearby.

To get there, take Freeway 17 south to Fremont, go left on Stevenson Blvd., right on Fremont Blvd., left on Washington Ave., and right on Mission Blvd. at Mission San Jose. Take the next left after the entrance to Ohlone College and park to the left. A staging area is planned nearby. The preserve may also be entered from Stanford Ave.

off Mission Blvd. near the Weibel Winery. From the Fremont BART Station, AC Transit bus #24 will take you to the preserve entrance at Ohlone College.

Mission Peak Trail *6.9 mi. round trip/2200 ft. climb*

This is a fairly strenuous hike, though not terribly long and it is certainly well worth the exertion. For those not up to such effort, the first part of this route is a pleasant walk, as are other trails in the hills near the college.

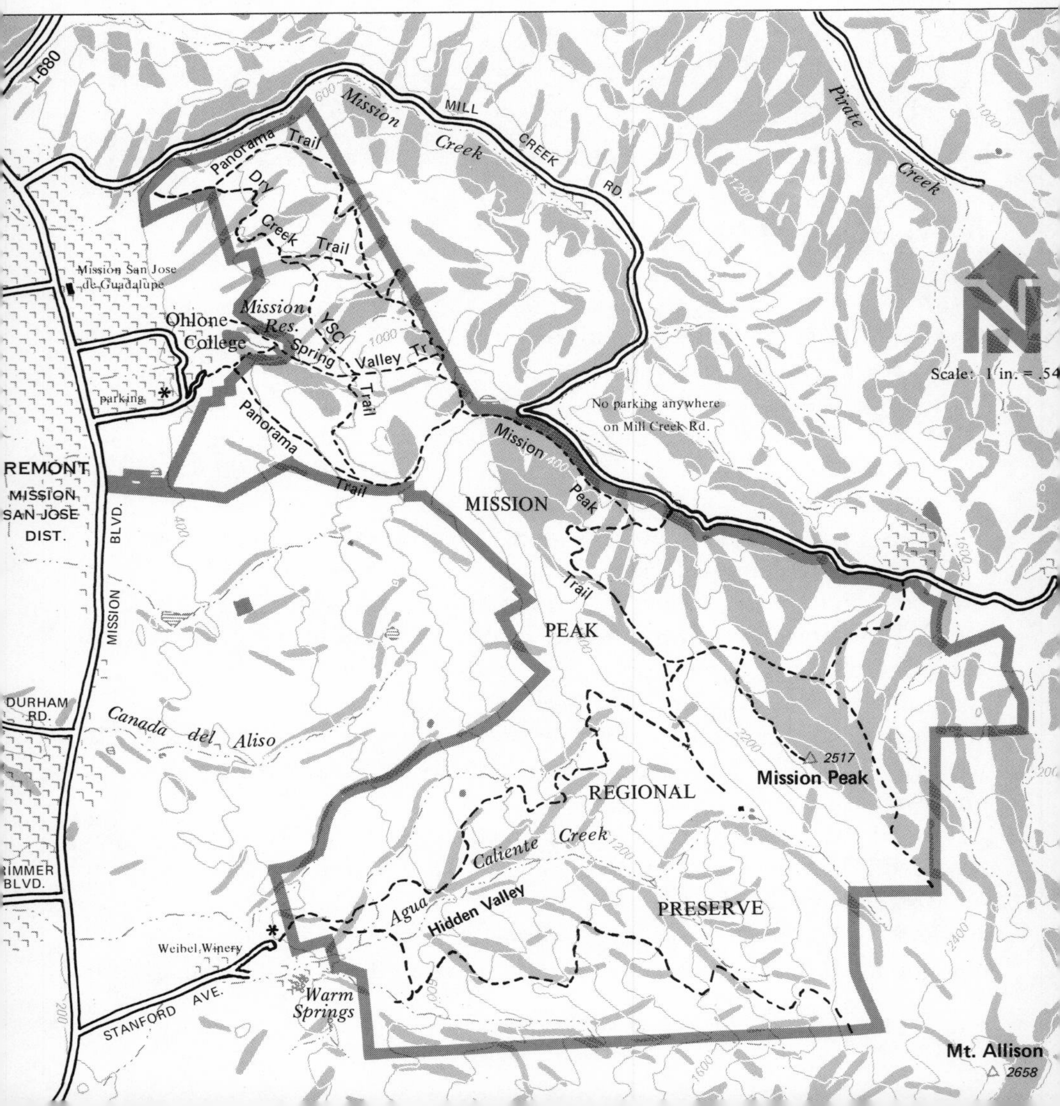

Goats, Mission Peak

From the parking lot, walk east past the swimming pool and cross a gate. Follow the trail along the fence to the right, the Panorama Trail, and gradually climb along the hillside and into a little ravine. Turn right onto the Misison Peak Trail and parallel Mill Creek Road through willows and brush (no parking anywhere on Mill Creek Rd.). Turn right on a dirt road, climbing to a broad ridgetop, then left, up around the corner of a fence line, and on up a steep rocky path to the top. Return by the same trail.

Mission Peak from Stanford Ave. *6.0 mi. round trip/2200 ft. climb*

From the preserve entrance at the end of Stanford Avenue, follow the dirt road which switchbacks up the steep west side of the peak. Turn left in a hanging valley beneath the peak's west face, climb to the ridge, and turn right on the Mission Peak Trail for the final pitch to the top. There is also a jeep trail up the spur south of Hidden Valley from which you can go cross-country to the peak.

Lake Elizabeth

This fair-sized lake in the middle of Fremont's Central Park is a nicely landscaped spot for many activities. You may sail or row on it, picnic and play on its shores, swim in a sandy beached lagoon, or jog the 2.2 mile path around the lake.

Near Little Yosemite

Sunol

Sunol Regional Wilderness is a beautiful area of high oak studded hills, colorful cliffs and cascading waters. It is located in the northern foothills of a very wild part of the Diablo Range, on Alameda Creek which rises far back in the mountains and is the largest stream in the East Bay. The hills rise nearly 2000 feet above the valley, their rounded grassy forms broken here and there by ancient rocks and groves of oak, bay, buckeye and sycamore lining the ravines reaching up their sides. Welch Creek Road cuts across the northern third of the park, below rocky Maguire Peaks. Along Alameda Creek there are picnic tables and wading pools, family campsites, and the green barn, the center for nature study programs. The rest of the park is "urban wilderness area," i.e., undeveloped grazing land. A well marked trail system covers the park. In the backcountry there are several backpacking campsites available by reservation–the only place you may backpack in the East Bay at this time.

To get there, take I-580 east, I-680 south, exit and go left on Calaveras Rd., turn left on Geary Road to the park entrance. To the left as you enter is a parking lot and the park headquarters. All of the following trails begin there. There are also a couple of spots along Welch Creek Rd. where you can park with prior arrangement and a permit.

Short Walks

The Shady Glen Trail winds through a little wooded ravine to make a ¾ mile loop. From park headquarters, cross the footbridge over the creek, turn right, then left up the Hayfield Road, go a few yards and turn left, finding the Shady Glen Trail leading up a little ravine, previously the site of an archery range. Come out on the Flag Hill Trail, turn left and return to the bridge.

There is also a short self-guided nature trail along the beginning of the Indian Joe Creek Trail and returning across the fields.

Little Yosemite *3.3 mi./400 ft. climb*

This fairly easy trail is one of my favorites. It climbs through oaks to the edge of the canyon of Alameda Creek, drops down to the beautiful boulders and cascades of Little Yosemite and returns along the creek.

From park headquarters, cross the footbridge and turn right along the creek. Go up the bank and turn right on the Canyon View Trail. Ascend this path up a rounded oak wooded ridge, cross a dirt road, and traverse the hillside. A few feet off the trail, a big rock protrudes out over the canyon, allowing a view straight down into the rocky gorge. Descend along the bottom of a wide hanging valley, go right on a dirt road and reach the Alameda Creek Road. A short path across the road leads down to Little Yosemite, where the creek cuts through a mass of ancient greenish rock, its layers contorted by millions of years of pressure deep in the earth. The creek cascades from pool to pool between 30 ft. rocks, sycamores and green grass. Follow the road down the canyon as it widens into the valley and walk through the picnic areas back to the starting point.

Flag Hill *3.5 mi./1000 ft. climb*

Flag Hill is the impressive eminence topped by a band of cliffs which stands north of the park entrance. The stiff climb to its summit rewards the hiker with a bird's eye view of the park.

From headquarters, cross the footbridge and turn left. Start up the hill, taking care to stay on the trail. Hikers taking shortcuts here have eroded the slope and confused the trails. Wind through oaks, traverse to the right below the cliffs, then cut back to the top of the hill. Enjoy the view from the edge of the cliffs and watch turkey vultures float by at eye level. From the trail sign, follow the dirt road north along the hill and descend to a crossroads by a big eucalyptus. Turn left on the Hayfield Road, pass a barn, the High Valley Camp, and wind down the hill through the hayfields back to the beginning.

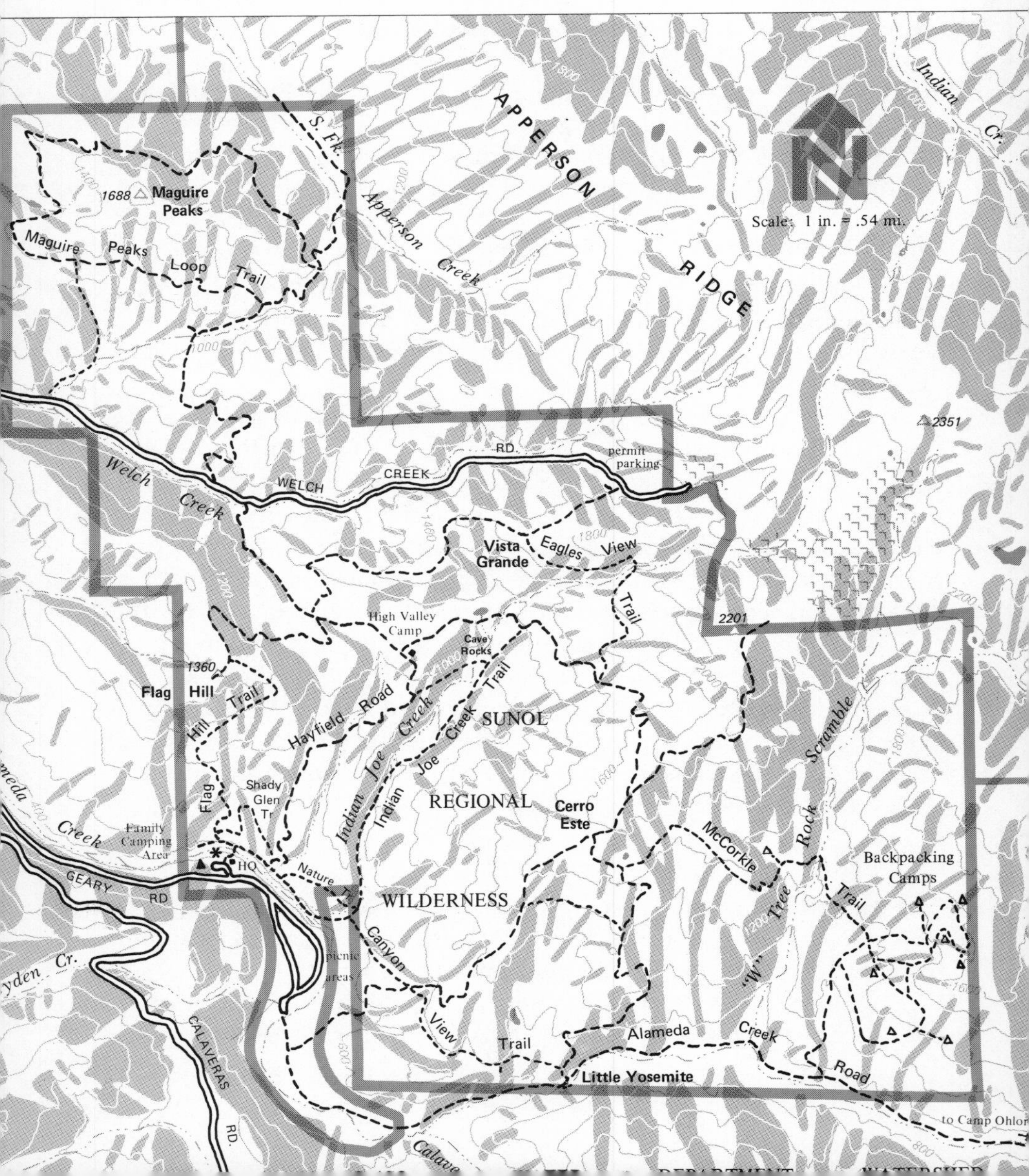

Indian Joe Creek & Eagles' View *5.3 mi./1400 ft. climb*

This is an especially nice route through some of the most beautiful parts of the park, along a sparkling little creek, past the interesting cave rocks, and along a high ridge with spectacular views. Much of it is on footpaths rather than dirt roads making it seem a little wilder than some of the other trails.

From the park headquarters, cross the creek and go right, then up the bank and turn left on the Indian Joe Creek Trail. Follow this creek as it winds gently between steep banks. As the slope steepens, leave the creek and climb through oak woodland. A sign points the way to the Indian Joe Cave Rocks, a pile of huge dark gray boulders enclosing cave-like spaces, a short ways off the trail to the left. Watch out for poison oak if you climb them. Continue up the trail, turn right on a dirt road, climb half a mile, then turn left on a footpath, the Eagles' View Trail. Cross meadows, then descend into the steep-walled ravine of Indian Joe Creek, the trail make of wooden steps in places. Cross the rocky cascading creek, climb the opposite bank, and traverse a steep hillside covered with sagebrush and wild oats. Look for Mariposa lillies in the spring. At the top of the hill, come to Vista Grande overlook, with a spectacular panoramic view. Turn left along the ridge and gradually descend through lots of spring wildflowers. Leave the ridge, drop to a crossroads, and turn left. Pass High Valley Camp and descend Hayfield Road to the park headquarters.

McCorkle Trail to Cerro Este *7.2 mi./1300 ft. climb*

This route follows Alameda Creek nearly to the eastern park boundary, then climbs through a beautiful little valley passing the backpacking camps, to Cerro Este, a high hill overlooking the park and surrounding hills.

From park headquarters, walk to the end of the picnic area and follow the Alameda Creek Road to Little Yosemite and beyond, where the valley becomes wide and flat, then narrows again. Turn left on the McCorkle Trail and climb to a valley dominated by a large rock piercing the gentle slopes. Circle through oaks and meadows above the valley, passing a network of short trails leading to backpacking campsites, and cross a rocky little creek. Climb a badly eroded hillside, covered with poppies in the spring, and traverse the hillside high above the canyon with red tailed hawks circling overhead. Near a small pond, turn right, leaving the McCorkle Trail. Climb steadily, turn right, and reach Cerro Este overlook where a wide panorama of surrounding hills presents itself. Descend to the left, overlooking the picnic areas far below. Wind down the hillside, through a shady little valley, crossing Indian Joe Creek, passing a pond and the High Valley Camp, and down the Hayfield Road back to park headquarters.

Maguire Peaks *9.2 mi./2200 ft. climb*

This route covers a lot of interesting and beautiful country. It is rather long, but rewarding, and is sure to be uncrowded. It could be made considerably shorter by starting from Welch Creek Road, but there is no parking allowed on this narrow country lane unless you make arrangements with the park district beforehand.

From park headquarters, cross the footbridge, go right, then left up the Hayfield Road, winding up past fields and grazing cattle to the High Valley Camp. Continue over the hill and descend through shady oak woodland to the bottom of a canyon and Welch Creek Road. Go left about 100 yards, then right, up a dirt road. Wind past a few redwoods, eucalyptus and cypress and contour around a grassy hill with the strong fragrance of sage. Now Maguire Peaks are in full view, showing outcroppings similar to those on Flag Hill. Descend into another oak wooded canyon, staying to the right, go upstream, and turn left on the Maguire Peaks Loop Trail. Traverse the north slope of the peaks through open oak woodland. Climb gradually around to the west slope, mostly bare grassland. Turn right and climb the northwest ridge to a view north of San Antonio Reservoir and bulging Apperson Ridge. Traverse down across the steep north slope covered with coyote bush and poison oak and level out around the east side of the peaks, again in oak woodland. Turn right and descend into the canyon to complete the loop. Retrace the now familiar trail back to park headquarters.

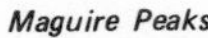
Maguire Peaks

Camp Ohlone

Camp Ohlone is a remote piece of EBRPD parkland seven miles up Alameda Creek from Sunol Regional Wilderness. It is available only for group overnight camping by advance reservation. Call 531-9043 weekdays, 9-4.

Shadow Cliffs

Shadow Cliffs Regional Recreation Area in Pleasanton is a former gravel quarry turned into a park with a lake for swimming, fishing and boating. The land was a gift of the Sand and Gravel Division of Kaiser Industries to the park district, who, with the help of funds from the U.S. Bureau of Outdoor Recreation, transformed the barren depleted quarry into a 90 acre lake and a nice park, which opened in 1971. More recently, facilities have been added to make the lake accessible to the handicapped. Along the shore are bicycle trails and picnic areas. A water slide is currently under construction.

To get there, take I-580 to Dublin, I-680 south, left on Bernal Ave., left on Main Street in Pleasanton, right on Stanley Blvd. to the park entrance.

Sycamore Grove

This 2 mile long park in Livermore along Arroyo Del Valle below the reservoir is a pleasant place for walking, riding or bicycling through the natural streamside environment. Ohlone Indians living nearby gathered acorns and seeds here, and many acorn grinding mortars have been found in the park. The area was also used for vineyards and gravel mining before the Livermore Area Recreation and Park District purchased the land in 1974. The LARPD provides naturalist programs for the public on a scheduled basis or by special arrangement for groups. Call 447-7300.

To get there, take I-580 to Livermore, go right on N. Livermore Ave., right on Stanley Blvd., left on Arroyo Rd., and right on Wetmore Rd. to the park entrance.

Livermore Bicycle Trail

A four mile off-road bicycle trail built by the City of Livermore and the Livermore Area Recreation and Park District facilitates cross-town transportation as well as providing a nice place for recreational bicycling. The trail extends from East Stanley Blvd. to Almond Ave. School, with trail connections to the Lawrence Livermore Laboratory.

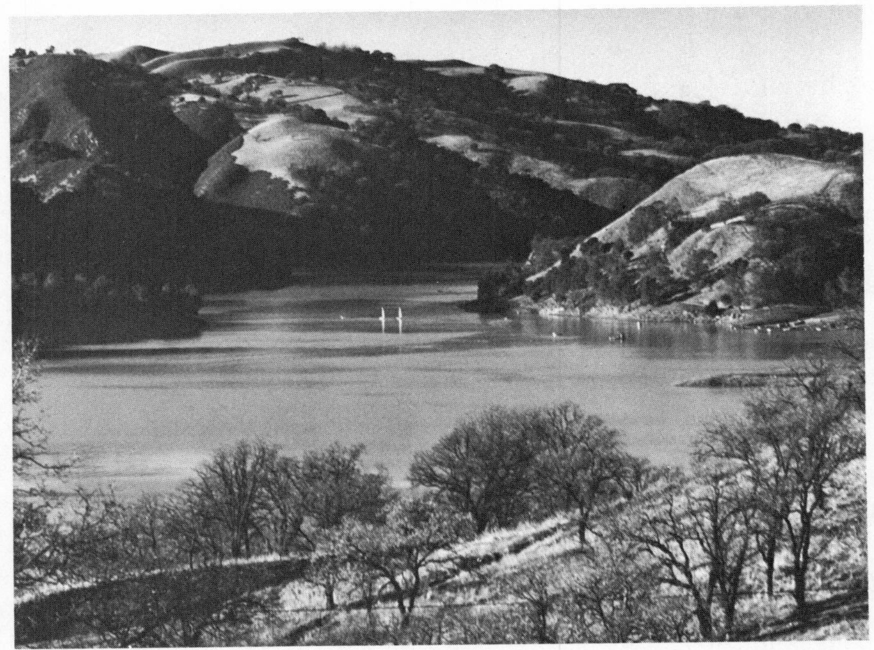

Del Valle Reservoir

Del Valle

Del Valle State Recreation Area is a large reservoir which is operated by the East Bay Regional Park District. It is located in the northern part of the large wild area south of Livermore. The dam floods the valley of Arroyo Del Valle, one of the largest streams draining the mountains to the south, and it is much like Alameda Creek in Sunol. The surrounding landscape is similar too, high oak wooded hills rising steeply from the valley, scattered digger pine and chaparral on the slopes and sycamores along the creek.

The favorite activities here are swimming, boating, fishing and camping. There is a nice sandy beach for swimming which is very popular on hot days. Boats are available for rent and there is a launching ramp for your own boat (10 m.p.h. speed limit). The lake is stocked with catfish, black bass and trout. There is a beautiful family camping area at the upper end of the lake near the creek, as well as several campgrounds for youth groups. There are also some nice hiking and riding trails.

To get there, take I-580 to Livermore, go right on N. Livermore Ave. which turns into S. Livermore Ave., then Tesla Rd. Turn right on Mines Rd. and go right again on Del Valle Rd. to the reservoir.

For a long interesting back road, stay on Mines Road, which follows the canyon of Arroyo Mocho south to San Antonio Valley, then heads west, climbing to the summit of Mt. Hamilton and Lick Observatory, then descends into San Jose.

Near the campground there is an interesting short nature trail which winds up the hillside opposite the campground entrance.

There are hiking trails following both the east and west shores from the head of the lake. These trails through unspoiled woods and grassland provide views of the lake and access to its shores for fishermen.

Another interesting trail begins at the west side of the bridge over the creek, where it enters the lake. Go past the service area and follow trail signs over rolling oak woodland and grassland and along a small creek to the highway, which you follow back down to the bridge.

Parklands in Land Bank

Several areas of undeveloped land, mostly in southern Alameda County, have been acquired for parks but have not been opened to the public because development is needed to make them accessible, safe, etc. I only mention them here to let you know that you may look forward to some day enjoying these areas and by no means suggest that you try to hike there now.

Ohlone Regional Wilderness is a large area of high wild ridges, nearly as high as Mt. Diablo, that are located between Sunol Regional Wilderness and Del Valle Reservoir. A trail is planned through this area connecting the two parks, a trail which would give its future users a wilderness experience of a quality not yet possible in the East Bay.

The EBRPD also owns a couple of other land bank parks in the area, the Bishop Ranch southwest of San Ramon, and the Tassajara Creek area near Santa Rita. Other EBRPD land bank areas include Brooks Island in the bay near Richmond, Browns Island in the river near Pittsburg, and several other pieces along the bay shore.

The city of Pleasanton parks department owns land on Pleasanton Ridge, a very beautiful area which will also be open for our enjoyment some day.

5. Mt. Diablo & Vicinity

Shell Ridge

This beautiful area of rolling oak wooded hills dominated by a steep hogback ridge, the western foothills of Mt. Diablo, would have been just another Walnut Creek housing development if it hadn't been for the foresight of that community's citizens. In the early 70's, they petitioned for a referendum which overturned the city council's commitment to development of the area, adopted a new plan, formed a new county service area, and approved a $6¾ million bond issue to buy the land. The result is much more than a community recreation area becoming popular with hikers, runners and equestrians; it is quite a special place, a fine natural area to be valued by the whole Bay Area.

Shell Ridge Recreation Area is also the western gateway, by trail, to Mount Diablo. Sharing the eastern boundary of Shell Ridge is undeveloped Diablo Foothills Regional Park, which in turn adjoins recent additions to Mt. Diablo State Park. These parklands make a wide swath of open land from quite near downtown Walnut Creek to the big wild area of Mt. Diablo. Running through these hills is the Briones to Mt. Diablo Trail, which is unofficially complete now from Shell Ridge to the mountain.

Shell Ridge is geologically a continuation of the Black Hills of Mt. Diablo, a set of vertically tilted layers of sandstone filled with fossil shells, a formation that was long ago the bottom of a shallow sea, and which also appears in many other places in the East Bay.

The recreation area is completely undeveloped except for trails. There are no restrooms or drinking water. Walnut Creek also has three other open space areas, Sugarloaf to the south, Acalanes Ridge to the west, and Lime Ridge to the northeast. In the future, all of these areas will be interconnected by trail.

To get to Shell Ridge, take Freeway 24 to Walnut Creek, go north on I-680 and take the first exit, Ygnacio Valley Rd. Go east about a mile and turn right on Homestead, then left on Marshall Dr., and go to the end of the street and the entrance to the open space area.

View from Briones to Mt. Diablo Trail

Horseshoe Pond Loop *2.8 mi./400 ft. climb*

This route is an easy loop around a portion of Shell Ridge, through rolling grassland and oak woodland and passing a fair-sized stock pond. There are supposed to be some Indian bedrock mortars on a knoll near the pond, but they escaped my casual search.

From the end of Marshall Dr., traverse left across the hill to a gap in the ridge and go to the right, climbing along the northwest slope above several backyards. Turn left when Horseshoe Pond comes into view, go down to it, scramble down the bank, across the dam and up the opposite hill a short distance. Turn right on a dirt road and wind gently up the hill, pass a trail branching left, and then turn left along Shell Ridge's northeast slope again. Turn right and go through a gap in the ridge, from which a side trip may be made up the steep hillside to the right to the top of the ridge and a panoramic view. Back on the southwest slope of the ridge, turn right on the Briones to Mt. Diablo Trail and wind down a gentle valley back to the trailhead.

Briones to Mt. Diablo Tr.—to Green Valley

4.8 mi./900 ft. climb eastbound, 400 ft. westbound—to jct. with trail from Green Valley Rd.

Though not yet officially open, you can now go by trail through Shell Ridge Recreation Area, through Diablo Foothills Regional Park and into Mt. Diablo State Park. The way leads through many miles of wild ranchland, much of the way between ridges and shut off from sight and sound of nearby urban areas. If you don't have the energy for this whole section of trail, the first part of it in Shell Ridge is an easy, pleasant walk for as far as you feel like going.

From the end of Marshall Dr., follow the trail up the gentle valley through grass and oaks and grazing cattle. A trail branches right and

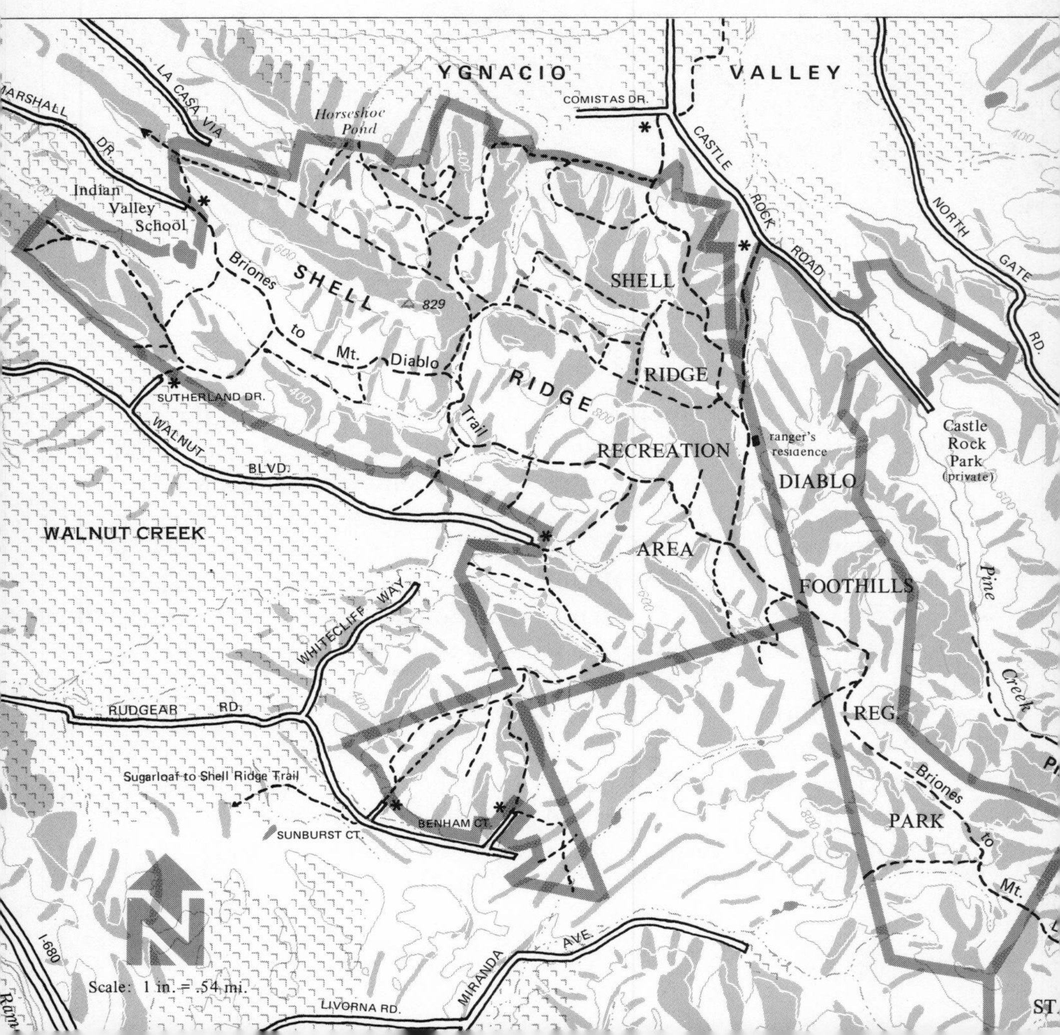

another left through a gap in the ridge. Go down around a hill, pass a pond, and come to a sign indicating a trail branching right to Sugarloaf Recreation Area. Continue until the dirt road curves to the left and the ranger's residence comes into view below. Cross the gate to the right, entering Diablo Foothills, and continue around the north side of the ridge, then through a low gap back to the south side and to the left up a treeless valley. A short side trip up the ridge on the left presents a view of the sandstone monolith, Castle Rock. Continue southeast into the State Park and through a couple of little valleys, to a fork at the northern rim of Green Valley. To the right leads down .8 mile to the trailhead at the end of Green Valley Road. To the left, the Briones to Mt. Diablo Trail continues up the mountain (see p. 111).

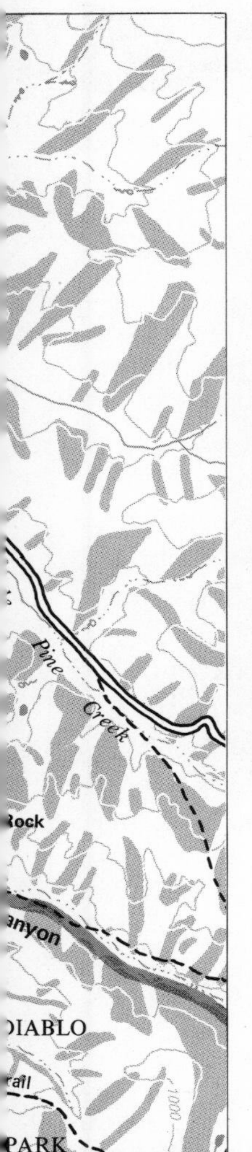

Castle Rock and Mt. Diablo

Mt. Diablo from Briones

Mount Diablo

The massive bulk of Mount Diablo dominates the view from much of the East Bay, rising high above the surrounding hills and valleys, long fingers of oak wooded ravines reaching up soft grassy slopes, big splotches of dark, velvety chaparral and rugged red-brown rock. From its summit on a clear day is visible one of the world's most extensive views, including Sierra peaks up to 300 miles away. For this reason, it was selected as the base point for the surveying of northern California in 1851.

Many myths are connected with the mountain. The Ohlone Indians of the Bay Area regarded it as a place of power, the residence of spirits. They believed that in the beginning there was a great flood and only Mt. Diablo stood above the water. Coyote, the only living thing, stood there on the mountain and one day saw floating on the water a feather which turned into Eagle. Later they were joined by Hummingbird, the flood subsided, and the three set out to create the human race. Eagle told Coyote how to find a woman and to marry her. After several comical attempts and a second wife, Coyote managed to people the earth.

The Spanish and Mexican settlers were also superstitious about the mountain. There are several versions of how it was named; the following is the one reported by General Mariano Vallejo:

"In 1806 a military expedition from San Francisco marched against the tribe 'Bolbones,' who were encamped at the foot of the mount; the Indians were prepared to receive the expedition, and a hot engagement ensued in the large hollow fronting the western side of the mount. As the victory was about to be decided in favor of the Indians, an unknown personage, decorated with the most extraordinary plumage and making divers movements, suddenly appeared near the combatants. The Indians were victorious and the incognito 'Puy' [evil spirit] departed towards the mount. The defeated soldiers, on ascertaining that the spirit went through the same ceremony daily and at all hours, named the mount 'Diablo,' in allusion to its mysterious inhabitant . . ."

Though it has mistakenly been described by many as a volcanic cone, the mountain is actually a large block of colorful metamorphic Franciscan rock which has been punched up through the overlying sedimentary beds, turning up steeply inclined layers of sandstone on the southwest and northeast.

Because of the relatively infertile soil and the elevation (3849 ft.), the vegetation is somewhat different from the surrounding hills–digger pine, scrub oak and juniper are common here as well as the familiar oaks, bays, chaparral and grassland. Many kinds of manzanita make their home here, including some found nowhere else.

During the height of the drought in 1977, a rare summer thunderstorm set a fire which consumed the whole north side of the mountain. Fires like this are a natural part of the ecology, clearing away overgrown brush, necessary for the seeds of some species to sprout, and replenishing minerals in the soil with ashes. The burnt area has already naturally reseeded itself and has begun its recovery, though it will be many years before it approaches its former botanic glory. Right after the fire, a local drive raised $15,000 to re-seed the area. When informed by naturalists that re-seeding was not necessary, the money was used to build a trail around the summit of the mountain, appropriately called the Fire Ecology Trail.

The top and south slope of the mountain were made a State Park in 1931. Recent acquisitions have expanded the park a good deal, but large areas of the mountain remain in private hands and there is much pressure to develop these lands. Homes are now being built in the southern foothills by the Blackhawk development despite a hard-fought battle by citizens to prevent it (despite the encroachment, the park has gained acreage in the Black Hills deeded by Blackhawk). Other developments threaten the sides of the mountain, especially in the Clayton area. A group called "Save Mt. Diablo" is dedicated to keeping the mountain in its natural state by opposing developments on it and encouraging purchases by the state. They can use your support and can be reached at P.O. Box 25, Concord, CA 94522.

In the last few years, the state has been so busy with expansion of the park that it has unfortunately been unable to keep up with trail maintenance in many places. The fire has not helped matters either. You may find that trails are poorly signed, hard to follow, or blocked by fallen trees. Some of the trails shown on the map have been developed and used primarily by horsemen's groups for trail rides, and are sometimes little more than cross country routes. However, of the trail routes described below, all are on wide fire roads or well used trails and should present no problems (with the exception of the Middle and Eagle Peak Trails which could use some work).

The state park is somewhat more uptight in their management than the regional parks, especially concerning dogs, which are not allowed on any trails. There are several nice areas for family camping, organized group camps and many picnic areas. On Sunday afternoons the roads are usually crowded with picnickers and sightseers, but not many venture onto the trails. Mt. Diablo is the only accessible place in the East Bay that usually gets some snow in the winter. After a good storm, when the top half of the mountain is white, cars jam the roads as people swarm to play in the snow. At the other extreme, the mountain is one of the hottest places in the region in the summer.

To get there, take Freeway 24 to Walnut Creek, then either: a) take I-680 north, Ygnacio Valley Rd. several miles, turn right on Walnut Ave., then right on North Gate Rd., or b) go south on I-680 to Danville, go left on Diablo Rd. for several miles and turn left on Mt. Diablo Scenic Blvd. which becomes South Gate Rd. Just beyond the North Gate, the two roads join and the Summit Road continues a couple of miles to the top where there is a stone lookout tower, or c) for the trails in the Clayton area, take Ygnacio Valley Rd. about 7 miles, turn right on Clayton Rd. about a mile and turn right on Mitchell Canyon Rd., which leads to a park entrance.

Short Walks

The Fire Ecology Trail is an easy ¾ mile loop of the top of the mountain from the lower summit parking lot. It offers breathtaking views in all directions (even better than the summit because the foreground is rugged rock and scrub oak, not a concrete wall). You can see how the vegetation is recovering from the 1977 fire which burnt over most of this area, sparing patches of chaparral here and there. The trail is currently being widened to make it wheelchair accessible. Find the trail to the left (north) across the Summit Road from the lower summit parking lot.

Rock City, near the South Gate, is a fascinating place to wander. Paths wind among huge blocks of sandstone carved with wind caves. Between the rocks grow oaks and manzanita. One path leads north along the crest of the hill then down to the west to Sentinel Rock, a prominent pinnacle with steps cut so you can climb to its top.

A scenic fire road in the Rock City area, the Fossil Ridge Trail, goes left from the road down to Live Oak Camp through shady oak woodland to a chaparral covered point overlooking Dan Cook Canyon and Danville (1.7 mi. round trip).

Another nice walk is the trail northwest from Juniper Camp, which after about ½ mile of breathtaking views to the west, comes to an equally impressive view north into Mitchell Canyon.

Briones to Mt. Diablo Tr.—to Rock City

.8 mi./200 ft. climb—Green Valley Rd. to jct. with Briones to Mt. Diablo Tr.; 3.3 mi./1100 ft. climb eastbound, 300 ft. westbound—from jct. to Rock City

This section of trail climbing into the Black Hills will reward the traveler with some very scenic country with a nice touch of ruggedness —steep hogbacks draped with chaparral, oaks and scattered digger pines, sandstone boulders jutting from their slopes.

Green Valley Road offers a convenient access point to the Briones to Mt. Diablo Trail a little more than midway between Shell Ridge (see p. 106) and Rock City. From the end of the pavement (not much room for parking) go through the gate and up the gravel road. Turn right just short of several buildings and climb around the side of a grassy hill. Turn right on the Briones to Mt. Diablo Trail (or continue on it from Shell Ridge) climb a little more, crossing Pine Ridge, and turn right again on the Wall Ridge Fire Trail (left goes into Pine Canyon). Climb rather steeply to the ridge. Stay to the left along the ridge crest above Emmons Canyon. Climb a little more to Wall Point and continue on the ridge, now above Dan Cook Canyon. Share the quiet with numerous hawks and vultures which soar nearby. A path branches to the right into the captivating outcrops of Rock City and shortly thereafter arrive at South Gate Road near the Rock City Picnic Area.

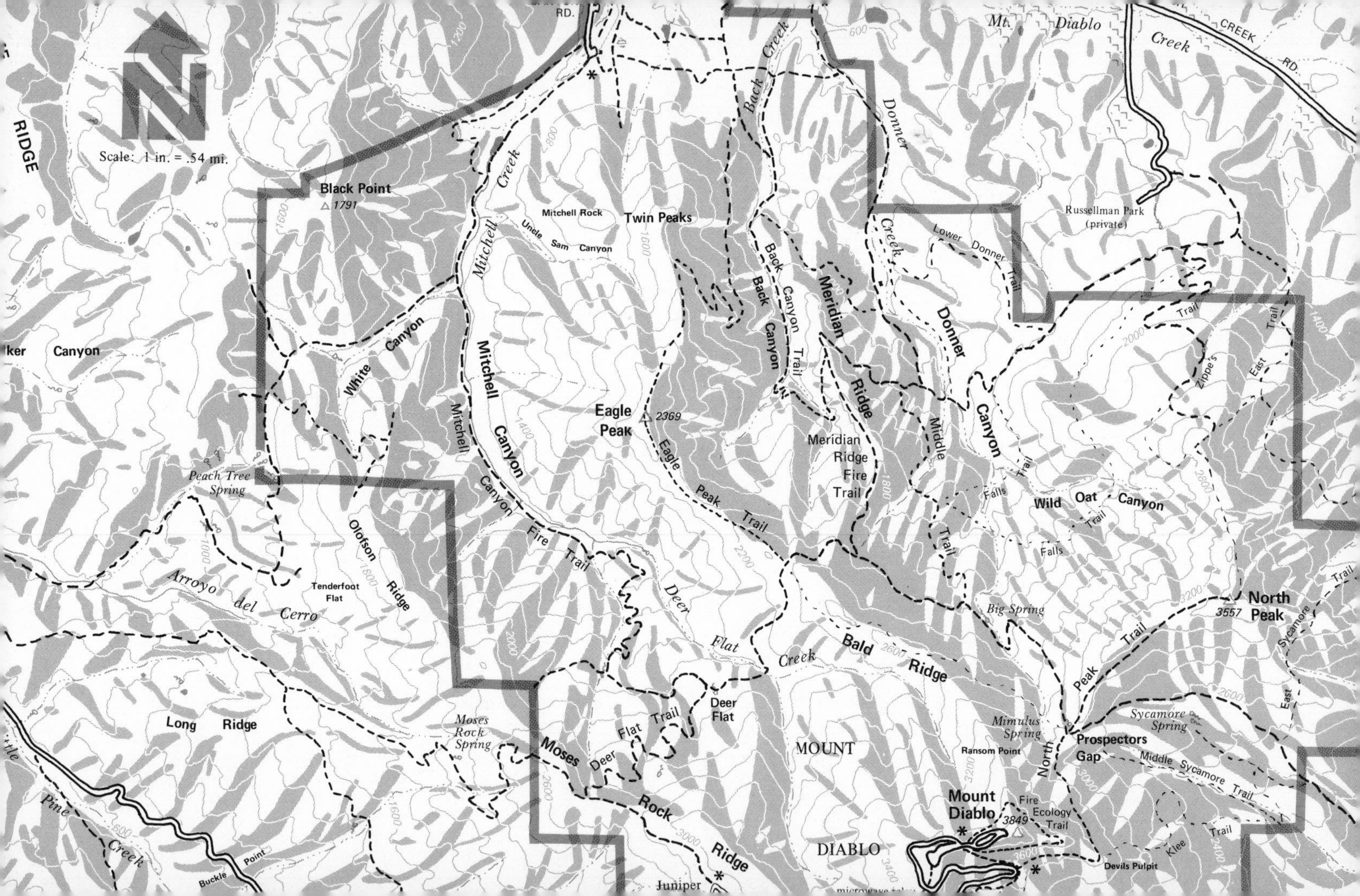
Scale: 1 in. = .54 mi.
Mt. Diablo Creek
CREEK RD.
RD.
Russellman Park (private)
Black Point 1791
Mitchell Rock
Twin Peaks
Uncle Sam Canyon
Mitchell Creek
Back Creek
Donner Creek
Lower Donner Trail
Back Canyon Trail
Back Canyon
Meridian Ridge
Donner Canyon
Middle Trail
Zippe's Trail
East Trail
White Canyon
Mitchell Canyon
Mitchell Canyon Fire Trail
Eagle Peak 2369
Eagle Peak Trail
Meridian Ridge Fire Trail
Wild Oat Canyon
Falls Trail
Peach Tree Spring
Olofson Ridge
Tenderfoot Flat
Arroyo del Cerro
Deer Flat Creek
Big Spring
North Peak 3557
Peak Trail
Sycamore
Bald Ridge
Deer Flat
Deer Flat Trail
Moses Rock Spring
Moses Rock Ridge
Long Ridge
MOUNT DIABLO
Mimulus Spring
Ransom Point
North Peak Trail
Prospectors Gap
Sycamore Spring
Middle Sycamore Trail
Mount Diablo 3849
Fire Ecology Trail
Klee Trail
Devils Pulpit
Juniper
Pine Creek
Buckle Point
Canyon
RIDGE

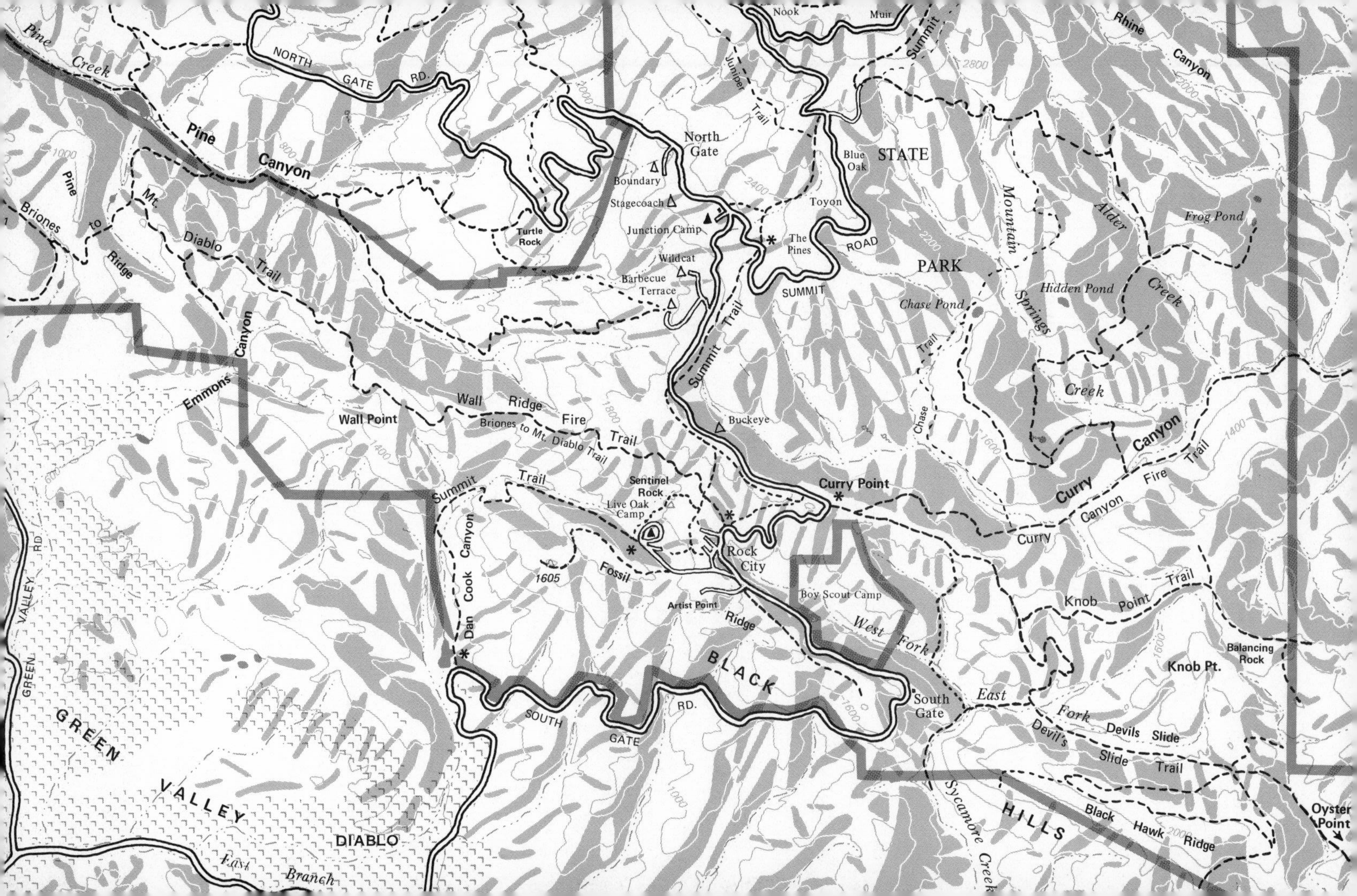

Pine Creek
NORTH GATE RD.
Nook
Muir
Summit
Rhine Canyon
Juniper Trail
North Gate
Blue Oak
STATE
Pine Canyon
Pine
Briones to Ridge
Mt. Diablo Trail
Boundary
Stagecoach
Junction Camp
Turtle Rock
Toyon
The Pines
ROAD
SUMMIT
Mountain Springs
Alder Creek
Frog Pond
PARK
Hidden Pond
Chase Pond
Wildcat
Barbecue Terrace
Summit Trail
Chase Trail
Creek
Emmons Canyon
Wall Point
Wall Ridge Fire Trail
Briones to Mt. Diablo Trail
Buckeye
Curry Canyon
Curry Canyon Fire Trail
Curry Point
Summit Trail
Sentinel Rock
Live Oak Camp
Rock City
Dan Cook Canyon
Fossil
1605
Artist Point
Ridge
Boy Scout Camp
West Fork
Knob Point Trail
Balancing Rock
Knob Pt.
BLACK
SOUTH GATE RD.
South Gate
East Fork
Devils Slide
Devil's Slide Trail
GREEN VALLEY RD
GREEN VALLEY
DIABLO
East Branch
Sycamore Creek
HILLS
Black Hawk Ridge
Oyster Point

Summit Trail *5.4 mi. one way/3200 ft. climb*

This trail is a steady climb from the base to the top of the mountain, making it a bit strenuous, but not exceedingly difficult (unless you pick a hot day). It crosses the road to the summit in several places, making it possible to use portions of the trail for shorter walks and providing water at picnic areas, making it unnecessary to carry a large canteen. In between crossings, it is relatively quiet and unspoiled and you get much more into the feelings of the mountain than you do from the road. Although you can see the same view from the summit by driving there, climbing the mountain on foot gives you a great feeling of accomplishment and lets you see the mountain's natural environment close up.

The Summit Trail begins at the mouth of Dan Cook Canyon on South Gate Road. This first section is one of the best parts of the trail, but since there is no good place to park there, Rock City is a more convenient and easier place to start, as it saves 1.8 mi. and 900 ft. of climbing.

For those starting at the bottom, the trail leaves the road to the left at a hairpin turn as the road just begins to climb from the valley. Walk through pleasant oaks into the mouth of the rugged canyon. Climb steadily up the wooded canyonside with scenes of bouldery chaparral on the far slope until you reach Live Oak Camp. Follow the road a short distance to Rock City Picnic Area.

From Rock City, go up South Gate Road a few yards to the next turn and find a couple of fire roads on the left. Follow the right hand one (the left is the Wall Ridge Fire Trail described above). Climb the grassy hillside and go left near Curry Point. Parallel South Gate Road, cross it, and continue climbing from grassland into chaparral and woods. Cross the Summit Road, pass a ranger's house, and climb steadily up a wooded ravine which becomes a steep grassy valley. Notice the convoluted layers of red-brown metamorphic rock exposed by the road cut. Cross the Summit Road again and follow a paved road to the site of Pioneer Camp. Go left on a trail up across the hillside scattered with pines and chaparral. Hear the shrill chirps of ground squirrels calling to one another, standing erect in front of their holes. Meet the Summit Road once more, but don't cross it. Traverse and climb to the right, coming to the hairpin turn where the North Peak Trail begins. Climb toward the summit and reach the end of the trail at the lower summit parking lot. Follow the road to the right to the lookout tower.

Hikers on trail from Juniper Camp

Curry Canyon

4.0 mi. round trip/800 ft. climb—to park boundary in Curry Canyon

From Curry Point, where the South Gate Road doubles back along a ridge above Rock City, several trails fan out into the very interesting country of the southeast corner of the park. The one into Curry Canyon is the left fork a short distance from the parking area. Follow the canyon, gradually winding down beside an oak shaded tributary of Marsh Creek to the park boundary. From that road, a path, the Chase Trail, and several roads, lead north up the side of the mountain to three ponds, and eventually connect with the Summit Road at what used to be Pioneer Camp.

Devil's Slide & Oyster Point

7.6 mi. round trip/2200 ft. climb—to Oyster Point
4.8 mi. round trip/1000 ft. climb—to top of Devil's Slide

This route leads through a fascinating landscape of rolling grassland and oak woodland, shady canyons, and chaparral cloaked cities of wind-carved sandstone more fanciful than Rock City.

From Curry Point take the right fork and follow the grassy crest of the ridge. After nearly a mile, turn right and descend into a canyon (a left takes you further along the ridge in chaparral, not far from the pinnacles of Knob Point and one of the East Bay's rare groves of Knobcone pine). At the bottom, turn left, cross the small creek and climb up the pretty little canyon called Devil's Slide. At the top there are several choices. The most travelled dirt road switchbacks sharply to the right and climbs along Black Hawk Ridge which overlooks the smooth rolling hills of the Tassajara area. Another trail climbs to the east end of that ridge. A trail to the left leads a short ways into a little valley rimmed with rocky outcrops which would make a great scene if it weren't for the power lines overhead.

To continue to Oyster Point, take the trail which goes straight ahead gently down through oak woodland, across a couple of little canyons, and up a ravine to a meadow where the trail ends. Climb the hill to the right to the grassy shoulder of Oyster Point, a nice spot to rest and enjoy the views all around. Return by the same route.

For a little variety on the way back, at the bottom of Devil's Slide, you may go left a little further down the canyon, then right on a path up the West Fork of Sycamore Creek, passing an odorous sulfur spring, and climbing to meet the fire road again on the ridge.

North Peak Trail *3.3 mi. round trip/1100 ft. climb*

Mt. Diablo's impressively rugged twin, North Peak, is the destination of this route. From the Summit Road's hairpin turn near the top of the mountain, follow a path, the North Peak Trail, across a steep slope below dark reddish crags, round the east ridge of the mountain and descend through shady woods and mossy rocks. From the saddle between North Peak and the main summit, Prospector's Gap, climb on a dirt road up the rugged slope, the last stretch very steeply, to the top of North Peak. Enjoy the spectacular view and return by the same route.

Around the North Side *6.0 mi./1800 ft. climb*

Before additions to the park made it accessible from Clayton, this route was the only way to the rugged north slope of the mountain. Now the trails from the Mitchell Canyon park entrance are a more interesting approach to this area, but this is still a good hike, though quite demanding, and it circles the whole north side.

From the lower summit parking lot, a trail descends just right of the antennae. Cross the Summit Road and continue down the ridge to Juniper Camp. Follow the Deer Flat Trail along Moses Rock Ridge, switchback down to Deer Flat, and turn right. Climb Bald Ridge and traverse across the mountainside. At Big Springs, begin climbing again, and push steeply up to Prospector's Gap. Turn right on the North Peak Trail and continue climbing around the east side of the mountain to the Summit Road. Go right on the Summit Trail back up to the parking lot.

The North Side

The north slope of the mountain is a wild, rugged area of bare red-brown rock, woods and chaparral, high ridges and deep canyons sweeping up from oak-dotted hills, gently rolling grassland, and splashing spring-fed creeks. It's a very different place from the cars and noise along the roads of the south side.

The landscape here was dramatically changed by the 1977 fire which burnt most of this side of the mountain. Where once grew impenetrable manzanita 10-15 ft. high, now there are bare blackened sticks with healthy tufts of new growth sprouting at their bases. In the spring, green grass and wildflowers cover the slopes, leaving only a few bare snags here and there as reminders of the fire.

The next three routes, which all start at the Mitchell Canyon park entrance, take you into this exceptional area and through its varied and impressive landscapes.

Mitchell Canyon to the Summit *6.3 mi. one way/3200 ft. climb*

This route is a wilder alternative to the Summit Trail for those wishing to climb the mountain by trail. A wide fire road leads along deep Mitchell Canyon and then climbs and climbs and climbs. The first couple of miles are nearly level, however, and make a nice leisurely walk.

From the Mitchell Canyon parking lot, take the middle of three roads and head into the canyon, passing a pond and following the creekside. A road branches right into White Canyon. Continue, passing the site of a former private park and begin climbing. Switchback steadily upward through oaks, pines and chaparral, looking back on the extremely rugged southwest face of Eagle Peak. At Deer Flat, turn right and keep climbing on the Deer Flat Trail. Finally, reach the grassy crest of Moses Rock Ridge and contour across its other side to the Summit Road at Juniper Camp. Find a path to the left from the camp entrance and climb back to the ridge and then along it. Cross the Summit Road next to a microwave tower and come out at the lower summit parking lot. Follow the road to the lookout tower at the very top.

Back Canyon & Donner Canyon *5.2 mi./1000 ft. climb*

This beautiful route leads through the whole range of north side terrain—from gently undulating grassland to steep chaparral—and along two lovely little creeks, a good, moderately strenuous excursion.

From the Mitchell Canyon parking lot, take the road to the left up the hillside a bit, then down and turn right, across the gentle grassy plain at the foot of the mountain. Turn right and head into the mouth of Back Canyon. The dirt road becomes a path along the creek, entering the burn area and re-crossing the creek several times. Climb through sprouting chaparral, circling up out of Back Canyon to Meridian Ridge. Turn left on the Meridian Ridge Fire Trail, go down the ridge a short way, and traverse, winding down into Donner Canyon. Turn left, down the canyon before reaching the creek, and leave the burn area at a cabin in a beautiful spot beside Donner Creek. Just above the cabin (which is occupied) turn left on a path which winds through pleasant oak woodland back to the mouth of Back Canyon. Return across the grassland to the parking lot.

North Peak from Eagle Peak

Middle Trail & Eagle Peak *8.4 mi./2300 ft. climb*

This route, in the same area as the previous one, goes higher and farther and tours the heart of this wilderness. It's a pretty strenuous hike, but the terrain is some of the most impressive in the region and yields some wonderful sights.

Start at the Mitchell Canyon parking lot and as above, take the left hand road up and down the hillside and across the plain. Keep going straight below the mouth of Back Canyon, cross Back Creek, and turn right on a dirt road beside Donner Creek, beautifully splashing over rocks in sunny oak woodland. Gently climb up into Donner Canyon, pass the cabin and continue steeply up to the Meridian Ridge Fire Road. Turn right, go about a quarter mile, and turn left on a narrow path, the Middle Trail. Climb steadily through burned and re-growing chaparral and pine snags. A faint path branches left, the Falls Trail, which leads to the seasonal waterfalls of Wild Oat Canyon coming down the cliffs, in view across the canyon as is all of the precipitous west face of North Peak. Continue climbing, going around one rounded spur after another and finally reach a fire road just west of Big Spring. Turn right and contour across the mountainside to Murchio Gap in Bald Ridge. Turn right on a rough path along the ridge, descending some, then climbing steeply to the top of Eagle Peak. Unlike most of the high points of the region, here there are no antennae or other artifacts of man, just rock, grass and junipers dropping away a couple of thousand feet on three sides and the Bay Area spread around the horizon. Continue, descending the ridge on the other side of the peak on a rather weak trail. At a point where the ridge levels off before the cliffs of Twin Peaks, switchback to the right, traversing the slope through burnt chaparral and pine snags, make a couple more switchbacks, passing near an old mine prospect in a ravine, then making a long traverse down into Back Canyon. Pass the few survivors of the Twin Peaks grove of Coulter Pines, and come out onto the flat grassland to meet the Back Canyon Trail. Return to the parking lot.

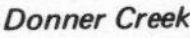
Donner Creek

Oil Canyon Loop Trail

Black Diamond Mines

The lonely windswept hills between Mt. Diablo and Antioch are quiet now, populated only by a few cows and hikers. With the exception of a tiny cemetery, a few piles of multi-colored earth, and tunnels hidden here and there in the rugged ravines, there is nothing here to tell of the bustling coal mining towns that stood here a hundred years ago. Other western mining towns become ghost towns when the mines shut down; here, the towns vanished leaving scarcely a trace. Gone are the homes of the thousands of Welch, Irish and Pennsylvanians, the miners working in more than a dozen mines, and the three railroads which carried coal down to the paddle wheeled steamers on the San Joaquin River. This area is still fascinating to visit, perhaps more so because it leaves so much of its story to one's imagination. And there are many miles of hiking trails in the rugged hills and gentle valleys, among the colorful sandstone outcrops, blue oaks, coulter pines, manzanita and waving fields of grass that make up Black Diamond Mines Regional Preserve.

The story of Black Diamond Mines begins about 50 million years ago, when the sea level fluctuated over a flat plain here, alternately flooding it and depositing sand, and retreating to allow swampy vegetation to grow in the warm, moist climate. Over a great many years, later deposits forced these beds down to a depth of about a mile where the sand was pressed into sandstone and the plants became coal. When Mt. Diablo punched up its core of ancient rock a few miles away, these beds were bent up at a steep angle toward the mountain, and were eroded until the coal and sandstone were exposed. This coal is very young as coal goes, and it is the softest type, lignite, which is inferior to harder coals.

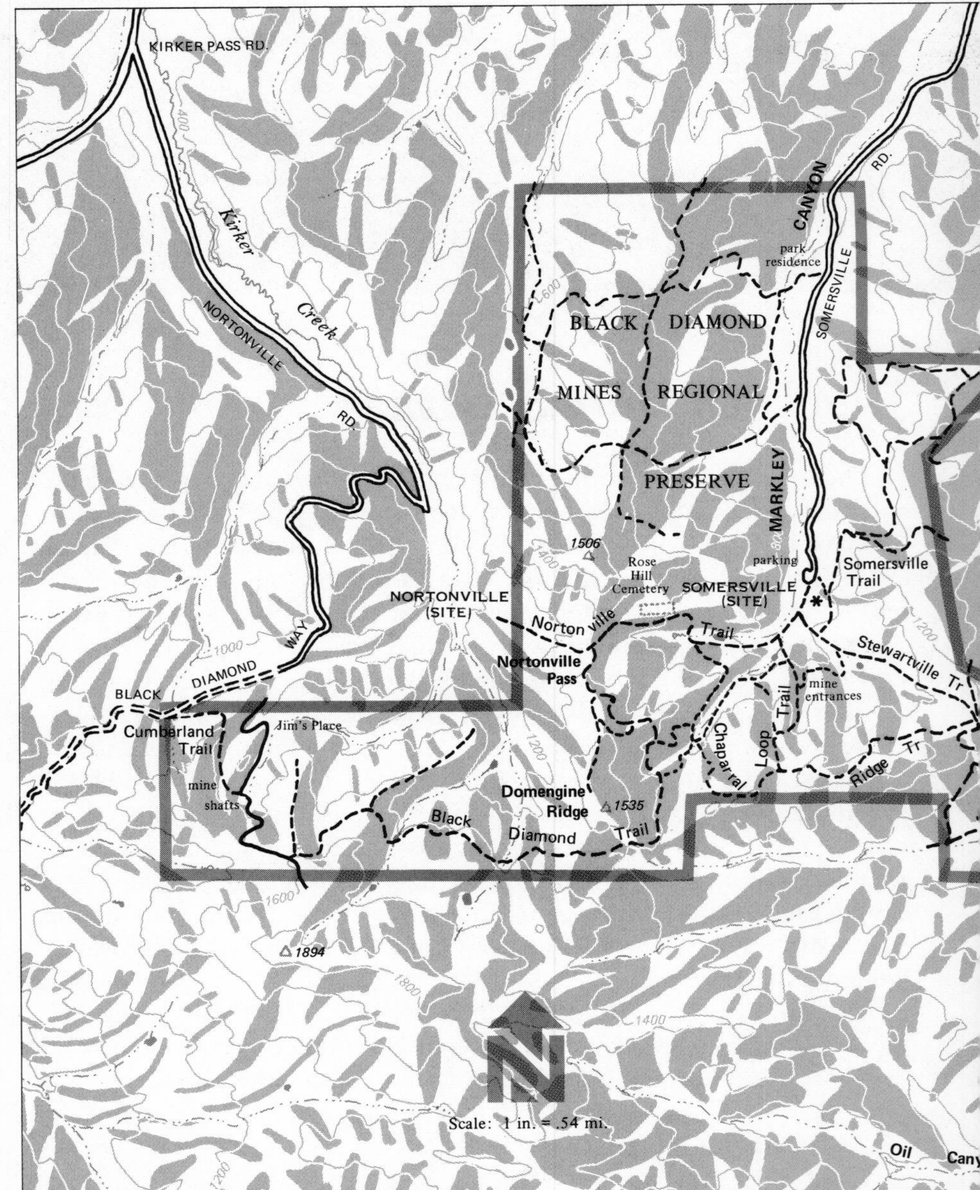

It was the presence of coal here that soon brought the attention of the Californians, who actually did more prospecting for coal than for gold in the early years. Coal was essentially the only energy source besides muscle power at that time. It ran river steamers, trains, mine machinery, and heated city buildings. Before local sources were found, it had been expensively shipped half way around the world.

Coal was discovered here in 1848, but the mines really got going when a couple of rich mines were found in the late 1850's. During its

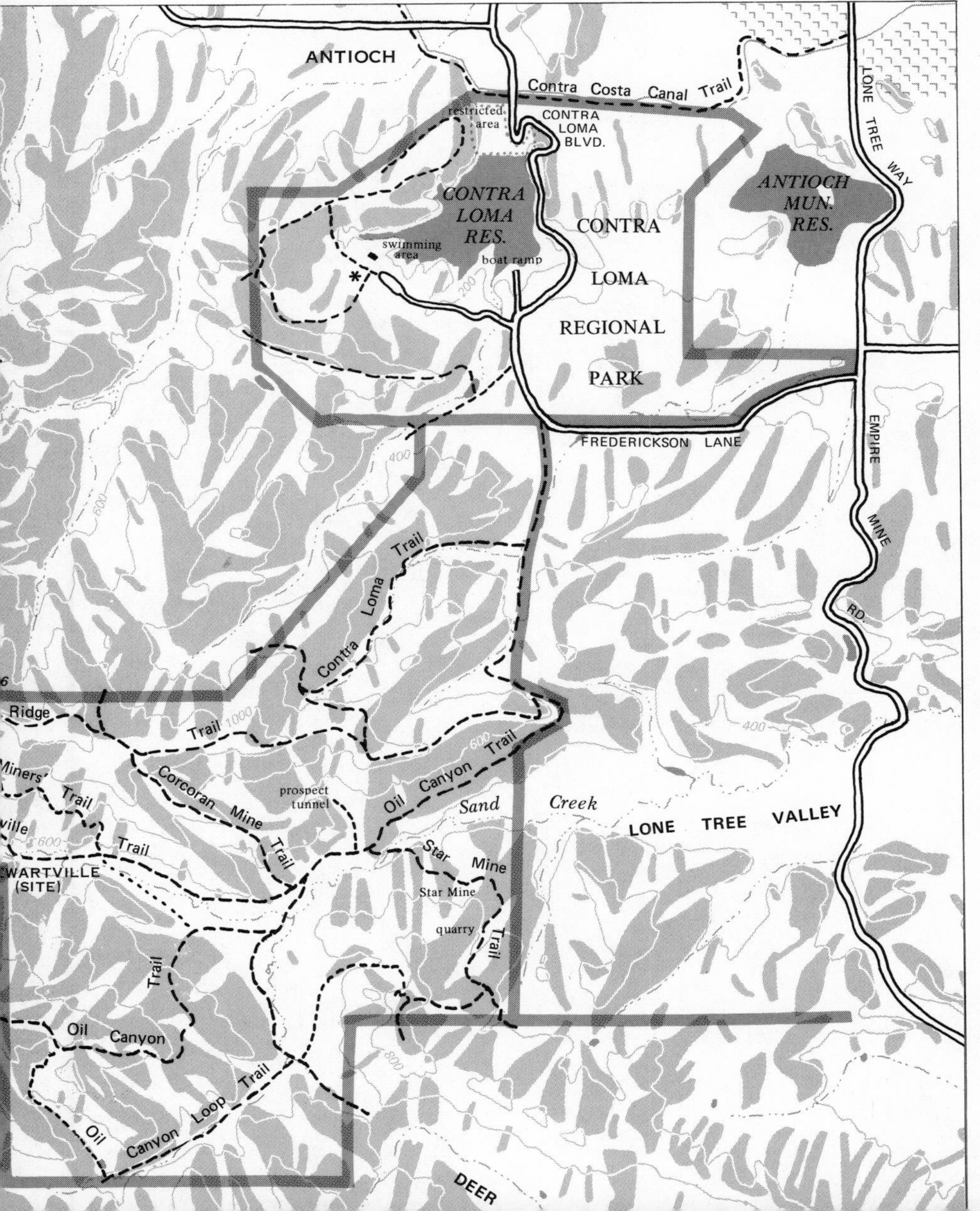

boom years, this region was the major source of coal in California. Over a million tons of coal valued at $20 million were taken from the mines before the last of them shut down in 1902, victims of competition from mines in the Pacific Northwest. The mines were reopened from 1922 to 1949 to mine silica sand which was good for making glass and foundry casings.

Unlike most early California mining towns, life was relatively peaceful here except for fires and mine explosions. A large number of the miners were Welch immigrants and life in Nortonville and Somersville was apparently much like that of the Welch villages they came from.

The acquisition of this land by the East Bay Regional Park District was not a simple matter. Shortly after they purchased it in 1964, it was discovered that it included 360 acres of federal land previously claimed under an 1872 mining law. The claimant, Steven Kosanke, planned to strip mine for silica sand. Fortunately, in 1972, with the help of several environmental groups, the park district was able to block the claim and obtain the land, and in 1976 the Preserve was opened to the public.

To get there, take Freeway 24 east, I-680 north, 24 through Concord, and east on Highway 4. Exit on Somersville Road in Antioch and go south up Markley Canyon to the parking lot at the site of Somersville.

The Mines

Although the Preserve abounds with interesting features of the natural world, most visitors' first interest is in the mines. The way to see them is to make reservations (phone 757-2620) for one of the history tours which are led by park staff on weekends for a nominal fee. The sights of the huge sand mine chambers, coal seams and fossils, as well as the colorful story beyind them, is an experience that shouldn't be missed. Be sure to call well in advance.

If you wish to do a little exploring underground on your own, there are several open tunnels which may be reached from the trails described below.

Mine Entrance

Short Walks

A gentle half-mile climb up the road will bring you to the Rose Hill Cemetery. Despite extensive vandalism, it is still a fascinating and picturesque spot, a place to stir the imagination with scenes from the past.

Another short walk takes you a short way up the Stewartville Trail, where a path goes to the right, along the base of the hills, making a short loop to the mine openings.

Chaparral Loop *1.7 mi./500 ft. climb*

This trail climbs a short but steep half-mile up the ravine directly south from the parking lot, passing the mine openings and taking you to the top of the ridge with good views of Mt. Diablo and all around. Scattered in the chaparral are Coulter pines, this area being the northern limit of their range. The large excavation to the left on the way up was made in the 50's to close a mine following an accidental death there. Turn right (west) along the ridge, then down into another ravine, the trail narrowing to a path. Trails branch left connecting with the Black Diamond Trail. Descend the ravine, and complete the loop.

Black Diamond Trail *6.6 mi./1500 ft. climb*

This route leads to the site of the largest former mine, the Black Diamond. Along the way are many views of the old townsites, the hills and the flat delta country beyond.

Follow the Nortonville Trail up past the cemetery to Nortonville Pass (or shortcut via the Chaparral Loop Trail). Turn left on the Black Diamond Trail which winds up and around a hill with a striking line of sandstone cliffs, Domengine Ridge. A side trip to the top of this hill provides spectacular views. Cross a saddle and continue along the side of the ridge above a ravine leading down to Nortonville. After a trail branches right, climb to a high ridgetop and turn right on a paved road. Descend to the north and come to a fork. To the left is the Cumberland Trail leading down to the narrow unpaved Black Diamond Way between Nortonville and Clayton. To the right, the Black Diamond Trail continues on the paved road to the park boundary. Near the fork there are a couple of adits (horizontal mine tunnels) and an open air shaft. Down the Black Diamond Trail there is a little excavation known as Jim's Place, once used as a dwelling. Return by the same route.

Sand Creek, below Stewartville

Stewartville Loop *4.4 mi./1200 ft. climb*

This route takes you up on a high ridge with a fine view, then down into a valley past the remains of Stewartville and along a path once used by the miners going to and from the mines.

Follow the Stewartville Trail to the left just beyond the parking lot and climb steadily to Stewartville Pass. Go through the gate and turn left on the Ridge Trail, climbing to the ridge and traversing its north side with good views of Antioch. Turn right at a small pond onto the Corcoran Mine Trail and descend the rocky crest of a ridge to the valley. Turn right on the Stewartville Trail and go up the valley to the Stewartville site. Climb around the right side of the tailings of the Central Mine on the Miner's Trail and along the steep hillside on this narrow path. Rejoin the Stewartville Trail and climb over the pass and back to Somersville.

Star Mine & Oil Canyon *9.2 mi./2000 ft. climb*

This route tours the southeast end of the Preserve and features a couple of open mine tunnels and lots of beautiful country. I have included two loops, the Star Mine Trail and the Oil Canyon Trail, but you may find that just one or the other is enough for one day.

Follow the Stewartville Trail (described above) over the pass and past the townsite. The Corcoran Mine Trail branches left and the Oil Canyon Trail branches right. About ¼ mile further, a trail branches left, leading up a ravine to a 400 ft. deep prospect tunnel. Turn right at this junction, onto the Star Mine Trail, and climb around the hill, passing the entrance of the Star Mine, 100 ft. deep, one of the last operated in the area. Continue into a rocky little ravine past a quarry and up a spur to the top of a hill with a nice view. Turn right on a path which descends a grassy ravine to the valley. At the next junction, go straight ahead on the Oil Canyon Trail, a dirt road, and go up this remote canyon undisturbed by mining activity. Turn right at the Preserve boundary and follow a path up a little ravine through buckeyes and chaparral, then grassland. Near the top of the ridge, turn right on a dirt road and descend around the ridge and back to the valley. For a short-cut back to Stewartville, go left at some picnic tables under oak trees and follow the bed of the old railroad that once served Stewartville. Follow the Stewartville Trail back to Somersville.

Contra Loma Trail

4.5 mi. one way/600 ft. climb northbound, 1100 ft. southbound

If you can arrange a car shuttle, you can hike from Black Diamond Mines to adjoining Contra Loma Regional Park where you may finish with a swim in the reservoir (May through Sept.).

Start as for the Stewartville Loop described above, taking the Stewartville Trail, then left on the Ridge Trail. At the junction with the Corcoran Mine Trail, go straight ahead, continuing on the Ridge Trail for about a mile. Turn left on the Contra Loma Trail, descend a canyon, and go left on the road leading to the lake.

Contra Loma

The cool blue waters of Contra Loma Reservoir just south of Antioch are a welcome contrast to the surrounding dry, nearly treeless hills. Since 1968 it has provided recreation for swimmers, boaters, hikers and fishermen. It has a large swimming beach of trucked-in white sand, wheelchair accessible, and a solar powered bathhouse. A boat ramp provides access to the lake for boats 17 ft. or shorter, electric powered only. There are large picnic areas and the lake is stocked with many kinds of fish.

Morgan Territory

Morgan Territory

East of Mt. Diablo there is a high wild hill area of rugged rock and chaparral and gently rolling oak savannah overlooking the vast Central Valley. The heart of these dry hills is Morgan Territory Regional Preserve, an undeveloped and uncrowded park well suited for a few hours of exploration by foot or horseback.

To get there from the north, take Freeway 24 to Walnut Creek, I-680 north, Ygnacio Valley Rd. to Clayton, east on Clayton Rd. which turns into Marsh Creek Rd. About 5 miles from Clayton, turn right on Morgan Territory Rd. Just before the summit, turn left into the parking area next to the ranger's house. From the south, take I-580 to Livermore, north on N. Livermore Ave. 4 miles, then right on Morgan Territory Rd. and over the top to the parking area.

To the North End *6.4 mi. round trip/600 ft. climb*

From the rolling plateau country you can look down on the Central Valley and beyond to the Sierra on a clear day. Just head east a bit from the parking lot, then north. You have several choices of trails along the broad ridgetop, but as long as you stay on the ridge, they all will eventually take you to the northern boundary.

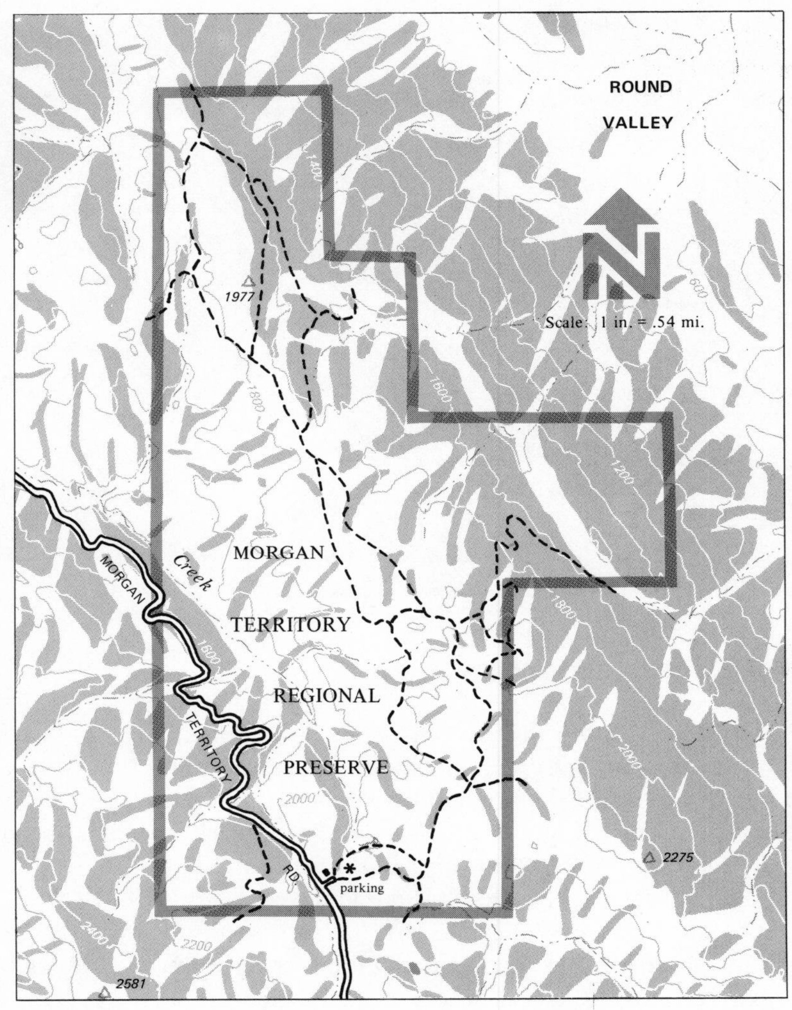
ROUND
VALLEY
Scale: 1 in. = .54 mi.
1977
MORGAN
TERRITORY
REGIONAL
PRESERVE
Creek
MORGAN
TERRITORY
RD.
parking
2275
2581
1400
1800
1200
2000
2200
2400
600

6. Watershed Lands

EBMUD Watershed

Two large watershed areas east of the Berkeley Hills are owned by the East Bay Municipal Utility District and have been left undeveloped to protect our water supply which is stored in five reservoirs there. For many years after the district's formation in 1923 these areas were closed to the public and most of us were unaware that here lay some of the wildest, most beautiful country of the East Bay. Then, in 1974, a system of trails through these areas was opened to the public, providing some wonderful new possibilities for hiking and riding. A little red tape is involved in their use, however, as you must first obtain a permit for a $5/year fee at one of the EBMUD offices, a measure which tends to limit users to those who are responsible area residents. Rangers patrol the area regularly and ask for permits to be shown. All of the trails may be used by either hikers or equestrians. Dogs are not allowed, nor is swimming in any of the reservoirs.

The northern of the two areas extends north from, and includes, San Pablo and Briones Reservoirs. Trails crossing this area connect Tilden Regional Park to Briones Regional Park and will soon be a link in a trail extending all the way from Tilden to Mt. Diablo and looping back through Las Trampas and Redwood Parks, the "Golden Loop." Parking is provided at three entrances to the trails, the Bear Creek Staging Area on Bear Creek Road opposite the entrance to Briones Regional Park, the Hampton Staging Area at the intersection of Bear Creek and Pinole Valley Roads, and Briones Overlook Staging Area on Bear Creek Road near Briones Dam. Inspiration Point in Tilden Park may also be used for parking and trail access.

The southern of the two areas extends east from Lake Chabot and Upper San Leandro Reservoir to the crest of Rocky Ridge, from Redwood and Anthony Chabot Regional Parks to Las Trampas Regional Wilderness. Trails crossing this area connect these parks and will also provide a link in the future "Golden Loop" trail which will soon extend from Mt. Diablo to the Skyline Trail in Redwood or Chabot. Trailheads are at the Valle Vista Staging Area on Canyon Rd. a mile south of Moraga, and the Chabot Staging Area on Redwood Road near Willow Park Golf Course in Castro Valley, the main entrance to Redwood Park, and at the end of Bollinger Canyon Road in Las Trampas. The first three trails described below are in the northern area and the last six routes are in the southern area.

Lafayette and San Pablo Reservoirs, also on EBMUD land, are covered on pp. 76-78. No trail permit is required for hiking on the trails of those areas.

Inspiration Trail to Briones Overlook

4.5 mi. one way/400 ft. climb eastbound, 800 ft. westbound

This route descends from the Skyline Trail in Tilden Park down the east slope of San Pablo Ridge to the upper end of San Pablo Reservoir and connects with either the Oursan Trail or Bear Creek Trail to link Tilden to Briones.

From Inspiration Point, go through the gate and follow the Inspiration Trail, a dirt road across the grassy hillside, come again to the ridgecrest across the fence from Nimitz Way, and turn right. Wind down the hill, pass a small pond, climb a knoll and descend a ridge. Cross San Pablo Dam Road and turn right on the Old San Pablo Trail, a paved road. Pass the EBMUD Forestry Headquarters and turn left on a narrow path, the Oursan Trail. Go through woods of oak and pine, cross San Pablo Creek, and turn back downstream along the opposite bank. Cross a temporary pipeline and come to the base of Briones Dam where the trail forks. The Oursan Trail branches to the left (p. 134). Go right on the Bear Creek Trail and climb the side of the spillway to the top of the dam and traverse the grassy slope to the Briones Overlook Staging Area.

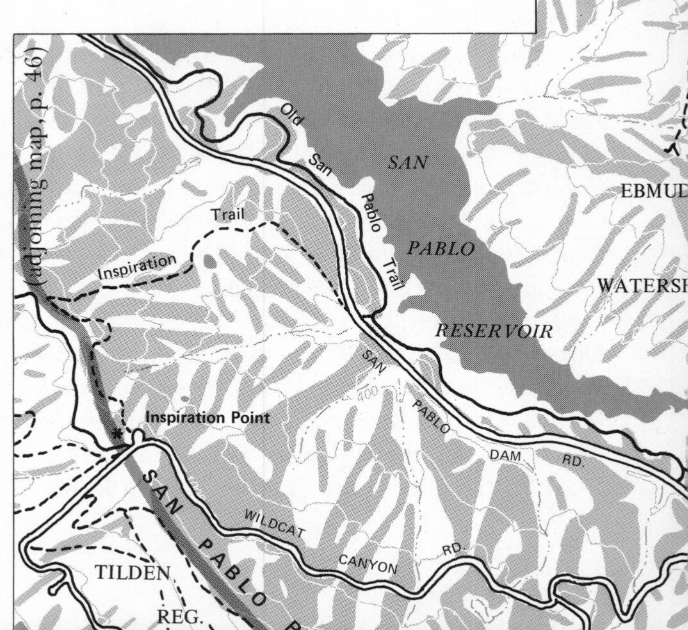

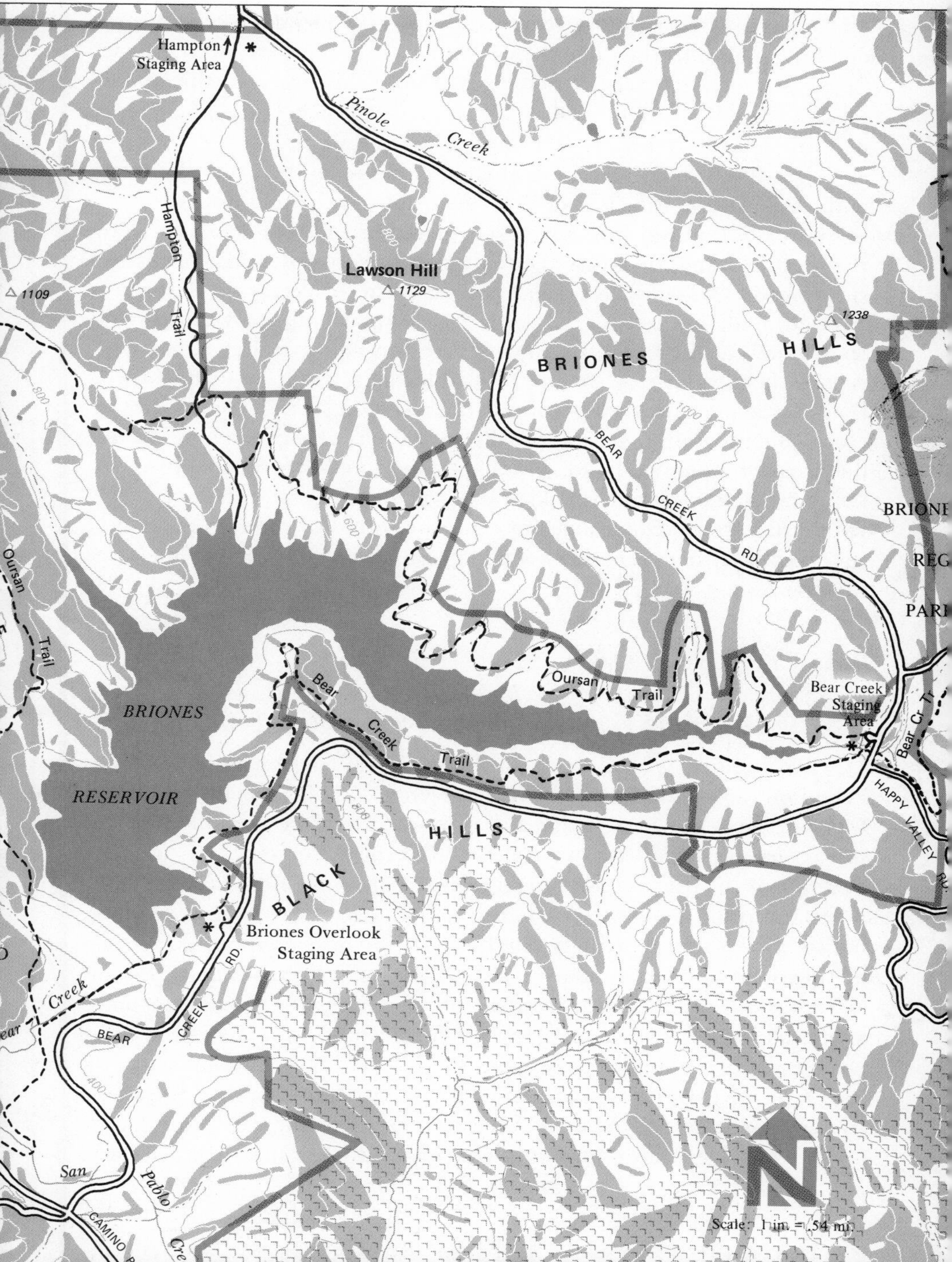

Hampton
Staging Area
Pinole
Creek
Hampton
Trail
Lawson Hill
1129
1109
1238
BRIONES
HILLS
BEAR
CREEK
RD.
BRIONE
REG
PARI
Oursan
Trail
BRIONES
RESERVOIR
Bear
Creek
Trail
Oursan
Trail
Bear Creek
Staging
Area
Bear Cr. Tr.
HAPPY
VALLEY
RD.
HILLS
BLACK
Briones Overlook
Staging Area
RD.
CREEK
BEAR
Creek
San
Pablo
CAMINO
Scale: 1 in. = .54 mi.

Oursan Trail

9.2 mi. one way/800 ft. climb eastbound, 800 ft. westbound

This trail circles around the northern side of Briones Reservoir, climbing high into the hills, then winding along the shore to the Bear Creek Staging Area. Of the two trails around the reservoir, this one is considerably longer and wilder. These two trails also make possible, for dedicated hikers, a big circle around Briones Reservoir.

From the Briones Overlook Staging Area, go south, cross the dam, and turn right on the Oursan Trail. Bear left, then right on a dirt road up a hill. Climb through grassland and brush, then level off along the crest of Sobrante Ridge. Dipping slightly, cross a saddle to the next ridge north, Oursan Ridge. Head back toward the reservoir, descend to a paved road, and turn right. To the left is the Hampton Trail which leads north to the Hampton Staging Area on Pinole Valley Road. Across the pavement, a short dirt road leads to the grave of Edward Hampton. Continue down towards the reservoir, turn left on a dirt road which winds inland a short distance then follows the long shoreline through oak woodland, winding in and out of the many coves. In the late fall the water is speckled with migrating geese and ducks. The far shore comes gradually nearer until the sound of running water in the trees says the reservoir has ended, and arrive at the Bear Creek Staging Area.

Bear Creek Trail

4.9 mi. one way/500 ft. climb eastbound, 300 ft. westbound– to Homestead Valley; 3.4 mi. to Bear Cr. Staging Area

This trail follows the southern shore of Briones Reservoir, winding in and out above the water in shady green woods. This is the preferred trail for travel between Tilden and Briones as it is the considerably shorter and easier of the two trails around the Reservoir.

From Briones Overlook Staging Area, follow the Bear Creek Trail north. Contour along the shore, through broadleaf evergreens overlooking the blue water, gradually climbing. At the big bend where the reservoir turns east, come out along a ridge, pass near the road, and contour again back in the woods, now gradually descending. The path becomes a dirt road which continues along the hillside and approaches the shore near the upper end of the reservoir. Cross level fields, and just short of Bear Creek Road, turn left. Here you have two choices: ford the creek and end up at Briones Staging Area, or continue along the south bank under the bridge if you intend to continue into Briones Regional Park.

If you have made the latter choice, follow the creek bank upstream along Happy Valley Road, cross the creek, and double back along the hillside into Briones Regional Park and beautiful broadleaf evergreen woods. Traverse high above Bear Creek, gradually climbing, and finally come out at Homestead Valley meeting the Homestead Valley Trail. This trail continues east to the Briones to Mt. Diablo Trail along Lafayette Ridge (see p. 75).

Redwood Trail

2.0 mi. one way/600 ft. climb eastbound, 600 ft. westbound

This trail connects the trail systems of Redwood Regional Park and the Skyline Trail with the Rocky Ridge Trail to Las Trampas Regional Wilderness.

From the main entrance parking lot in Redwood Park, go up the Canyon Trail and turn right on the East Ridge Trail. 50 yards beyond a clump of redwoods atop the second rise, turn right on a narrow path winding down through redwoods generously mixed with common companions—bay, madrone, alder and sword fern. Cross San Leandro Creek and the road at the junction of Pinehurst Road and Canyon Road. Traverse along the steep broadleaf evergreen wooded canyonside then out into brush and grass, turn left on a dirt road, and descend to Valle Vista Staging Area.

King Canyon Loop *6.2 mi./800 ft. climb*

This is a trail with beautiful woods, quiet pastoral scenes, and, with luck in the winter, great flocks of wild geese grazing on the hillsides and floating on the still waters of Upper San Leandro Reservoir.

Start at Valle Vista Staging Area and go left from the gate, through pine forest and across a bridge. Stay on the dirt road past farm houses, past the (temporary) Rocky Ridge Trail branching left, and up into tall bay trees passing a little hollow with giant ferns. Wind in and out of ravines that corrugate the hillside, in oak woodland overlooking the long narrow reservoir. Round a grassy hillside and head into a gentle valley, King Canyon. Come to a road and go left along the fence on the Rocky Ridge Trail. Cross a gully and follow tire tracks straight up a grassy hillside to the left which becomes a dirt road. Turn right (left soon reaches the hilltop with broad views), turn left and traverse the wooded hillside. Drop steeply, pass a house, and descend to the left, completing the loop.

Rocky Ridge Loop Trail *5.9 mi./2000 ft. climb*

This route climbs from Las Trampas Regional Wilderness over Rocky Ridge, along its west face below impressive sandstone cliffs, and back over the ridge again. It's a strenuous hike, much like the Devil's Hole route described on p. 85 but slightly longer. And like that route, it goes through some of the most inspiring scenery of the East Bay.

From the parking lot of Las Trampas at the end of Bollinger Canyon Road, go up the Rocky Ridge Road and left on the Upper Trail just as for the Devil's Hole route. At the crest of the ridge, cross the fence and go southwest along the ridge on the Rocky Ridge Loop Trail. Descend a dirt road down the spur north of Devil's Hole and turn right at the junction with the Ramage Peak Trail. Contour across the grassy slopes and wooded ravines along the base of the ridge, crossing several little creeks. Turn right on the Rocky Ridge Trail and climb steeply, round a spur and go left on the paved Rocky Ridge Road not far from the antennae at the ridge's summit. Descend back to the parking lot.

Rocky Ridge Trail

8.5 mi. one way/2400 ft. climb eastbound, 1900 ft. westbound

This somewhat demanding route goes from Valle Vista Staging Area across remote canyons and ridges to Las Trampas Regional Wilderness. Recent trail work has made it considerably easier to follow than it was previously. The scenery is pretty impressive.

From Valle Vista, go left through the pines, cross the bridge, and (temporarily) follow the King Canyon Loop Trail, a dirt road past farm houses. Turn left up the grassy hill, and pass another house. The Old Moraga Ranch Trail branches left. Go high along the hillside, descend, cross the road, go through a Christmas tree farm and up a gentle valley. Climb steeply out of oak woods and over the top of a grassy ridge. Traverse down the other side, cross Buckhorn Creek, and climb again to the next ridge. Turn left on a dirt road along the ridge. After the Rocky Ridge Loop Trail branches right, climb steeply over Rocky Ridge and go left on the Rocky Ridge Road down to the parking lot at the end of Bollinger Canyon Road.

Ramage Peak Trail

9.6 mi. one way/2700 ft. climb northbound, 1900 ft. southbound

This long and strenuous route goes from Chabot Staging Area through miles of wild and beautiful hills to Las Trampas. A lot of work has been done on this trail recently, and much of it has been re-routed.

West from Rocky Ridge,

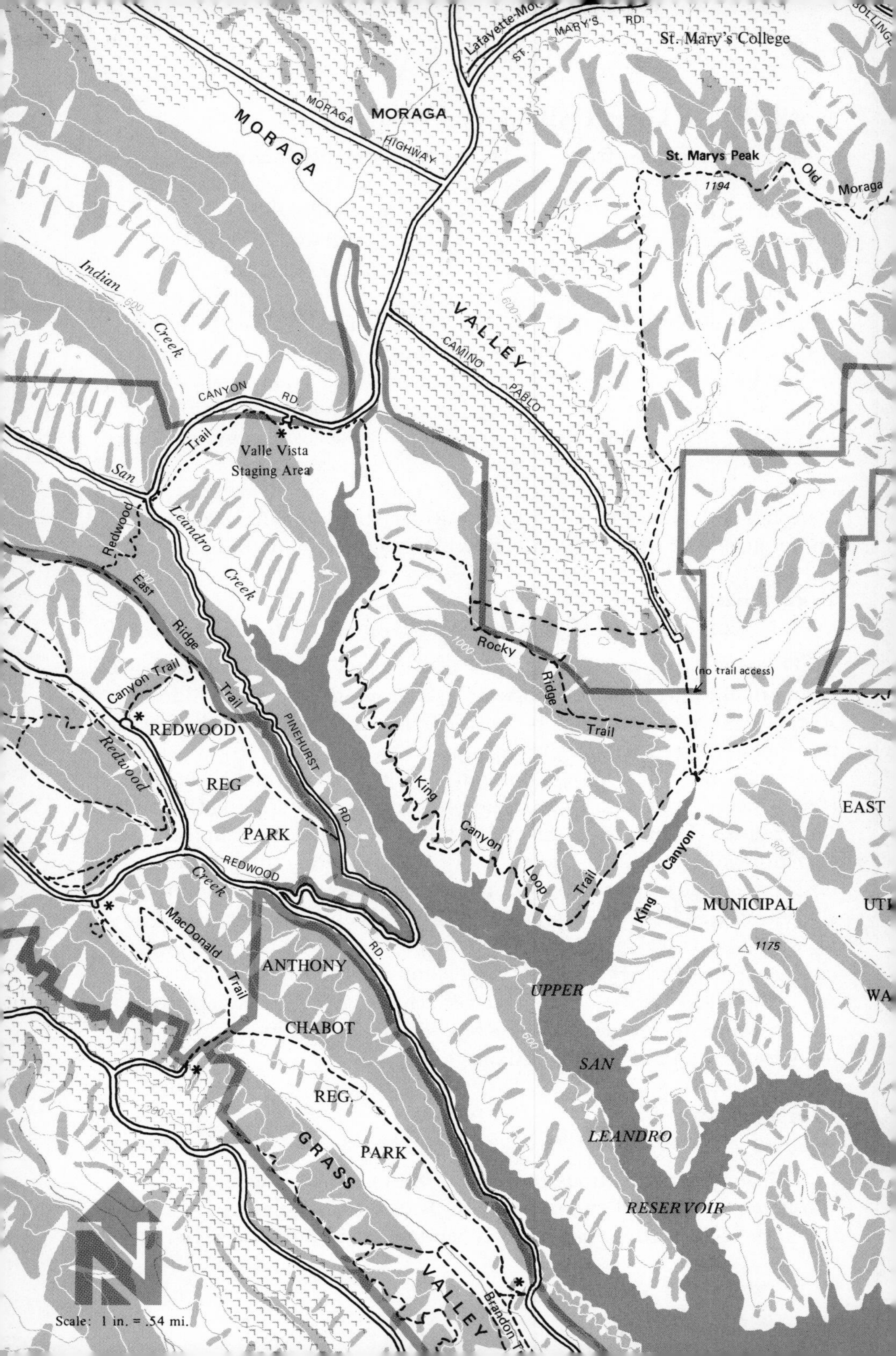

Lafayette-Mo
ST. MARY'S RD.
St. Mary's College
MORAGA
MORAGA
MORAGA HIGHWAY
St. Marys Peak
1194
Old Moraga
Indian Creek
600
VALLEY
CAMINO PABLO
CANYON RD.
Trail
Valle Vista
Staging Area
San Leandro Creek
Redwood
East Ridge Trail
Canyon Trail
REDWOOD
REG
PARK
Redwood
PINEHURST RD.
1000
Rocky Ridge Trail
(no trail access)
King Canyon Loop Trail
King Canyon
EAST
REDWOOD
Creek
RD.
MacDonald Trail
ANTHONY
CHABOT
REG.
PARK
MUNICIPAL
UT
1175
UPPER
SAN
LEANDRO
RESERVOIR
WA
GRASS
VALLEY
Brandon T
800
Scale: 1 in. = .54 mi.

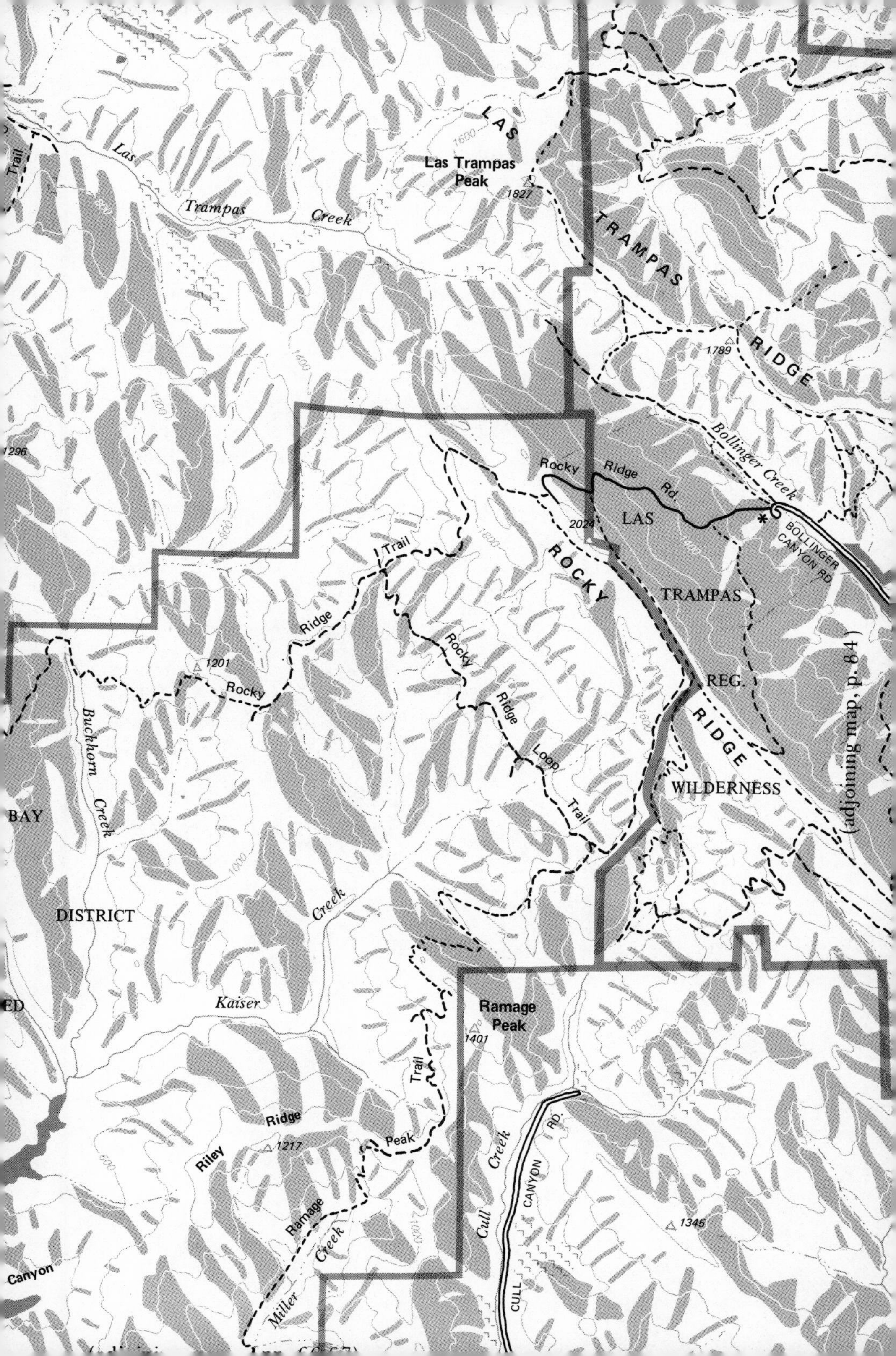

LAS TRAMPAS RIDGE
Las Trampas Peak
1827
Las Trampas Creek
Trail
800
1600
1400
1200
1296
1789
Bollinger Creek
Rocky Ridge Rd
2024
LAS TRAMPAS REG. WILDERNESS
BOLLINGER CANYON RD
ROCKY RIDGE
Trail
Rocky Ridge
1201
Rocky Ridge Loop Trail
(adjoining map, p. 84)
BAY
Buckhorn Creek
DISTRICT
1000
Creek
Kaiser
ED
Ramage Peak
1401
Trail
Ridge
Riley
1217
Peak
Ramage
600
Canyon
Miller Creek
Cull Creek
CULL CANYON RD.
1345

The new trail alignment is much more direct and saves nearly a mile and a half and 1000 feet of climbing. Work on it is not quite done yet, but it should be complete by the time you read this.

From Chabot Staging Area, cross the gravel road and follow a path through the Christmas tree farm, along a fence line, to the right of a corral and onto a dirt road along the base of the hill. As you head into a little canyon, go left on a path across a creek and switchback up the grassy hill to a transmission tower and contour. Go right on a dirt road a few yards, then left on the path again, traversing along the wooded hillside and into a little canyon. Cross a creek and continue to traverse around a wooded ridge. Go left on a dirt road a few yards, then right on the trail again. Cross Miller Creek, pass the old site of the Mendonca Ranch, and follow the creek upstream in beautiful woods. Climb through woods and brush to the grassy ridge and go right on a dirt road. Cross the west slope of Ramage Peak and climb a path to its

South from Rocky Ridge Trail

King Canyon Loop Trail

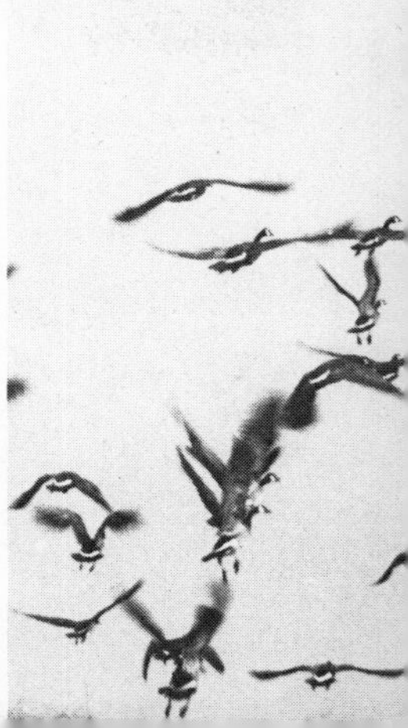

north shoulder. Descend steeply on a narrow path through dense oaks and bays, down a ravine, then up a grassy spur back to the ridge and road again. Turn right on the Rocky Ridge Loop Trail, climb the spur north of Devil's Hole over Rocky Ridge and follow the Rocky Ridge Road down to the parking lot at the end of Bollinger Canyon Road.

Moraga to Castro Valley

15.0 mi. one way/3100 ft. climb northbound, 2800 ft. southbound

This route is perhaps the ultimate in long trails through remote East Bay hills, and on foot it's a real bear. Once was probably enough for me, but don't let me discourage you because it's a beautiful trip to walk all day without roads, houses or people, to be far enough out in wild beautiful country that an occasional airplane is the only intrusion of civilization.

The components of this route have already been described in the above three routes. From Valle Vista Staging Area take the Rocky Ridge Trail, go right on the Rocky Ridge Loop Trail, right again on the Ramage Peak Trail, and end up at the Chabot Staging Area.

Deer, Ramage Peak Trail

Canada geese

Bibliography

Anderson, Don L., "The San Andreas Fault," *Continents Adrift* (Readings from *Scientific American*), W. H. Freeman and Co., 1972.

Baerg, Henry J., *How to Know the Western Trees,* Wm. C. Brown Co., 1955.

Bakker, Elna S., *An Island Called California,* University of California Press, 1971.

Berry, William D. and Elizabeth, *Mammals of the San Francisco Bay Region,* University of California Press, 1959.

California Department of Natural Resources, Division of Mines, Bulletin 154, *Geologic Guidebook to the San Francisco Bay Counties,* 1951.

Davis, Harold E., *A Short History of Contra Costa County,* San Ramon Valley Unified School District, 1965.

Diablo Press, *Diablo's Complete Guidebook to the East Bay and the University of California,* Diablo Press, 1962.

East Bay Regional Park District, Brochures of.

Ferris, Roxana S., *Native Shrubs of the San Francisco Bay Region,* University of California Press, 1968.

Howard, Arthur David, *Evolution of the Landscape of the San Francisco Bay Region,* University of California Press, 1962.

Margolin, Malcolm, *The Ohlone Way,* Heyday Books, 1978.

Sharsmith, Helen K., *Spring Wildflowers of the San Francisco Bay Region,* University of California Press, 1959.

Van der Zee, John, *Canyon: The Story of the Last Rustic Community in Metropolitan America,* Harcourt, 1972.

Bob Newey grew up in Richmond and Lafayette and has spent most of his life in the Bay Area learning to love its natural surroundings. He currently works as a graphic artist and lives in Hayward with his wife, Maureen, and their two sons.

Near Little Yosemite, Sunol